9/02

The Collected Works of
Langston Hughes

Volume 3

The Poems: 1951–1967

Projected Volumes in the Collected Works

Publication of

The Collected Works of Langston Hughes

has been generously assisted by

Landon and Sarah Rowland

and

Morton and Estelle Sosland

The Collected Works of

Langston Hughes

Volume 3

The Poems: 1951–1967

Edited with an Introduction
by Arnold Rampersad

University of Missouri Press
Columbia and London

Copyright © 2001 by Ramona Bass and Arnold Rampersad, Administrators
   of the Estate of Langston Hughes
Introduction and Chronology copyright © 2001 by Arnold Rampersad
University of Missouri Press, Columbia, Missouri 65201
Printed and bound in the United States of America
All rights reserved
5   4   3   2   05   04   03   02

Library of Congress Cataloging-in-Publication Data

Hughes, Langston, 1902–1967.
   [Works. 2001]
   The collected works of Langston Hughes / edited with an introduction
      by Arnold Rampersad.
      p.   cm.
   Includes bibliographical references and indexes.
   ISBN 0-8262-1339-1 (v. 1 : alk. paper)—ISBN 0-8262-1340-5
(v. 2 : alk. paper)—ISBN 0-8262-1341-3 (v. 3: alk. paper)
   1. African Americans—Literary collections.   I. Rampersad, Arnold, II. Title.
PS3515.U274   2001
818'.5209—dc21   00-066601

♾ This paper meets the requirements of the
American National Standard for Permanence of Paper
for Printed Library Materials, Z39.48, 1984.

Designer: Kristie Lee
Typesetter: BOOKCOMP, Inc.
Printer and binder: Thomson-Shore, Inc.
Typefaces: Galliard and Optima

Published by arrangement with Alfred A. Knopf, a division of Random House,
Incorporated.

Contents

Acknowledgments

The University of Missouri Press is grateful for assistance from the following individuals and institutions in locating and making available copies of the original editions used in the preparation of this edition: David Roessel; Anne Barker and June DeWeese, Ellis Library, University of Missouri–Columbia; Teresa Gipson, Miller Nichols Library, University of Missouri–Kansas City; Ruth Carruth and Patricia C. Willis, Beinecke Rare Book and Manuscript Library, Yale University; Ann Pathega, Washington University.

The *Collected Works* would not have been possible without the support and assistance of Patricia Powell, Chris Byrne, and Wendy Schmalz of Harold Ober Associates, representing the estate of Langston Hughes; of Judith Jones of Alfred A. Knopf, Inc.; and of Arnold Rampersad and Ramona Bass, co-executors of the estate of Langston Hughes.

Chronology

1902 James Langston Hughes is born February 1 in Joplin, Missouri, to James Nathaniel Hughes, a stenographer for a mining company, and Carrie Mercer Langston Hughes, a former government clerk.

1903 After his father immigrates to Mexico, Langston's mother takes him to Lawrence, Kansas, the home of Mary Langston, her twice-widowed mother. Mary Langston's first husband, Lewis Sheridan Leary, died fighting alongside John Brown at Harpers Ferry. Her second, Hughes's grandfather, was Charles Langston, a former abolitionist, Republican politician, and businessman.

1907 After a failed attempt at a reconciliation in Mexico, Langston and his mother return to Lawrence.

1909 Langston starts school in Topeka, Kansas, where he lives for a while with his mother before returning to his grandmother's home in Lawrence.

1915 Following Mary Langston's death, Hughes leaves Lawrence for Lincoln, Illinois, where his mother lives with her second husband, Homer Clark, and Homer Clark's young son by another union, Gwyn "Kit" Clark.

1916 Langston, elected class poet, graduates from the eighth grade. Moves to Cleveland, Ohio, and starts at Central High School there.

1918 Publishes early poems and short stories in his school's monthly magazine.

1919 Spends the summer in Toluca, Mexico, with his father.

1920 Graduates from Central High as class poet and editor of the school annual. Returns to Mexico to live with his father.

1921 In June, Hughes publishes "The Negro Speaks of Rivers" in *Crisis* magazine. In September, sponsored by his father, he enrolls at Columbia University in New York. Meets W. E. B. Du Bois, Jessie Fauset, and Countee Cullen.

1922 Unhappy at Columbia, Hughes withdraws from school and breaks with his father.

1923 Sailing in June to western Africa on the crew of a freighter, he visits Senegal, the Gold Coast, Nigeria, the Congo, and other countries.

1924 Spends several months in Paris working in the kitchen of a nightclub.

1925 Lives in Washington for a year with his mother. His poem "The Weary Blues" wins first prize in a contest sponsored by *Opportunity* magazine, which leads to a book contract with Knopf through Carl Van Vechten. Becomes friends with several other young artists of the Harlem Renaissance, including Zora Neale Hurston, Wallace Thurman, and Arna Bontemps.

1926 In January his first book, *The Weary Blues,* appears. He enrolls at historically black Lincoln University, Pennsylvania. In June, the *Nation* weekly magazine publishes his landmark essay "The Negro Artist and the Racial Mountain."

1927 Knopf publishes his second book of verse, *Fine Clothes to the Jew,* which is condemned in the black press. Hughes meets his powerful patron Mrs. Charlotte Osgood Mason. Travels in the South with Hurston, who is also taken up by Mrs. Mason.

1929 Hughes graduates from Lincoln University.

1930 Publishes his first novel, *Not without Laughter* (Knopf). Visits Cuba and meets fellow poet Nicolás Guillén. Hughes is dismissed by Mrs. Mason in a painful break made worse by false charges of dishonesty leveled by Hurston over their play *Mule Bone.*

1931 Demoralized, he travels to Haiti. Publishes work in the communist magazine *New Masses.* Supported by the Rosenwald Foundation, he tours the South taking his poetry to the people. In Alabama, he visits some of the Scottsboro Boys in prison. His brief collection of poems *Dear Lovely Death* is privately printed in Amenia, New York. Hughes and the illustrator Prentiss Taylor publish a verse pamphlet, *The Negro Mother.*

1932 With Taylor, he publishes *Scottsboro Limited,* a short play and four poems. From Knopf comes *The Dream Keeper,* a book of previously published poems selected for young people. Later, Macmillan brings out *Popo and Fifina,* a children's story about Haiti written with Arna Bontemps, his closest friend. In June, Hughes sails to Russia in a band of twenty-two young African Americans to make a film about race relations in the United States. After the project collapses, he lives for a year in the Soviet Union. Publishes his most radical verse, including "Good Morning Revolution" and "Goodbye Christ."

1933 Returns home at midyear via China and Japan. Supported by a patron, Noël Sullivan of San Francisco, Hughes spends a year in Carmel writing short stories.

1934 Knopf publishes his first short story collection, *The Ways of White Folks.* After labor unrest in California threatens his safety, he leaves for Mexico following news of his father's death.

1935 Spends several months in Mexico, mainly translating short stories by local leftist writers. Lives for some time with the photographer Henri Cartier-Bresson. Returning almost destitute to the United States, he joins his mother in Oberlin, Ohio. Visits New York for the Broadway production of his play *Mulatto* and clashes with its producer over changes in the script. Unhappy, he writes the poem "Let America Be America Again."

1936 Wins a Guggenheim Foundation fellowship for work on a novel but soon turns mainly to writing plays in association with the Karamu Theater in Cleveland. Karamu stages his farce *Little Ham* and his historical drama about Haiti, *Troubled Island*.

1937 Karamu stages *Joy to My Soul,* another comedy. In July, he visits Paris for the League of American Writers. He then travels to Spain, where he spends the rest of the year reporting on the civil war for the *Baltimore Afro-American*.

1938 In New York, Hughes founds the radical Harlem Suitcase Theater, which stages his agitprop play *Don't You Want to Be Free?* The leftist International Workers Order publishes *A New Song,* a pamphlet of radical verse. Karamu stages his play *Front Porch*. His mother dies.

1939   In Hollywood he writes the script for the movie *Way Down South,* which is criticized for stereotyping black life. Hughes goes for an extended stay in Carmel, California, again as the guest of Noël Sullivan.

1940   His autobiography *The Big Sea* appears (Knopf). He is picketed by a religious group for his poem "Goodbye Christ," which he publicly renounces.

1941   With a Rosenwald Fund fellowship for playwriting, he leaves California for Chicago, where he founds the Skyloft Players. Moves on to New York in December.

1942   Knopf publishes his book of verse *Shakespeare in Harlem.* The Skyloft Players stage his play *The Sun Do Move.* In the summer he resides at the Yaddo writers' and artists' colony, New York. Hughes also works as a writer in support of the war effort. In November he starts "Here to Yonder," a weekly column in the Chicago *Defender* newspaper.

1943   "Here to Yonder" introduces Jesse B. Semple, or Simple, a comic Harlem character who quickly becomes its most popular feature. Hughes publishes *Jim Crow's Last Stand* (Negro Publication Society of America), a pamphlet of verse about the struggle for civil rights.

1944   Comes under surveillance by the FBI because of his former radicalism.

1945   With Mercer Cook, translates and later publishes *Masters of the Dew* (Reynal and Hitchcock), a novel by Jacques Roumain of Haiti.

1947   His work as librettist with Kurt Weill and Elmer Rice on the Broadway musical play *Street Scene* brings Hughes a financial windfall. He vacations in Jamaica. Knopf publishes *Fields of Wonder,* his only book composed mainly of lyric poems on nonracial topics.

1948   Hughes is denounced (erroneously) as a communist in the U.S. Senate. He buys a townhouse in Harlem and moves in with his longtime friends Toy and Emerson Harper.

1949   Doubleday publishes *Poetry of the Negro, 1746–1949,* an anthology edited with Arna Bontemps. Also published are *One-Way Ticket* (Knopf), a book of poems, and *Cuba Libre: Poems of Nicolás Guillén* (Anderson and Ritchie), translated by Hughes and Ben Frederic Carruthers. Hughes teaches for three months at the University of Chicago Lab School for children. His opera about Haiti with William Grant Still, *Troubled Island,* is presented in New York.

1950   Another opera, *The Barrier,* with music by Jan Meyerowitz, is hailed in New York but later fails on Broadway. Simon and Schuster publishes *Simple Speaks His Mind,* the first of five books based on his newspaper columns.

1951   Hughes's book of poems about life in Harlem, *Montage of a Dream Deferred,* appears (Henry Holt).

1952   His second collection of short stories, *Laughing to Keep from Crying,* is published by Henry Holt. In its "First Book" series for children, Franklin Watts publishes Hughes's *The First Book of Negroes.*

1953   In March, forced to testify before Senator Joseph McCarthy's subcommittee on subversive activities, Hughes is exonerated after repudiating his past radicalism. *Simple Takes a Wife* appears.

1954   Mainly for young readers, he publishes *Famous Negro Americans* (Dodd, Mead) and *The First Book of Rhythms.*

1955   Publishes *The First Book of Jazz* and finishes *Famous Negro Music Makers* (Dodd, Mead). In November, Simon and Schuster publishes *The Sweet Flypaper of Life,* a narrative of Harlem with photographs by Roy DeCarava.

1956   Hughes's second volume of autobiography, *I Wonder As I Wander* (Rinehart), appears, as well as *A Pictorial History of the Negro* (Crown), coedited with Milton Meltzer, and *The First Book of the West Indies.*

1957   *Esther,* an opera with composer Jan Meyerowitz, has its premiere in Illinois. Rinehart publishes *Simple Stakes a Claim* as a novel.

Hughes's musical play *Simply Heavenly,* based on his Simple
character, runs for several weeks off and then on Broadway.
Hughes translates and publishes *Selected Poems of Gabriela Mis-
tral* (Indiana University Press).

1958   *The Langston Hughes Reader* (George Braziller) appears, as well
as *The Book of Negro Folklore* (Dodd, Mead), coedited with
Arna Bontemps, and another juvenile, *Famous Negro Heroes
of America* (Dodd, Mead). John Day publishes a short novel,
Tambourines to Glory, based on a Hughes gospel musical play.

1959   Hughes's *Selected Poems* published (Knopf).

1960   *The First Book of Africa* appears, along with *An African Trea-
sury: Articles, Essays, Stories, Poems by Black Africans,* edited by
Hughes (Crown).

1961   Inducted into the National Institute of Arts and Letters. Knopf
publishes his book-length poem *Ask Your Mama: 12 Moods for
Jazz. The Best of Simple,* drawn from the columns, appears (Hill
and Wang). Hughes writes his gospel musical plays *Black Nativ-
ity* and *The Prodigal Son.* He visits Africa again.

1962   Begins a weekly column for the *New York Post.* Attends a writers'
conference in Uganda. Publishes *Fight for Freedom: The Story of
the NAACP,* commissioned by the organization.

1963   His third collection of short stories, *Something in Common,*
appears from Hill and Wang. Indiana University Press publishes
Five Plays by Langston Hughes, edited by Webster Smalley, as well
as Hughes's anthology *Poems from Black Africa, Ethiopia, and
Other Countries.*

1964   His musical play *Jericho–Jim Crow,* a tribute to the civil rights
movement, is staged in Greenwich Village. Indiana University
Press brings out his anthology *New Negro Poets: U.S.A.,* with a
foreword by Gwendolyn Brooks.

1965   With novelists Paule Marshall and William Melvin Kelley,
Hughes visits Europe for the U.S. State Department. His gospel
play *The Prodigal Son* and his cantata with music by David
Amram, *Let Us Remember,* are staged.

1966   After twenty-three years, Hughes ends his depiction of Simple in his Chicago *Defender* column. Publishes *The Book of Negro Humor* (Dodd, Mead). In a visit sponsored by the U.S. government, he is honored in Dakar, Senegal, at the First World Festival of Negro Arts.

1967   His *The Best Short Stories by Negro Writers: An Anthology from 1899 to the Present* (Little, Brown) includes the first published story by Alice Walker. On May 22, Hughes dies at New York Polyclinic Hospital in Manhattan from complications following prostate surgery. Later that year, two books appear: *The Panther and the Lash: Poems of Our Times* (Knopf) and, with Milton Meltzer, *Black Magic: A Pictorial History of the Negro in American Entertainment* (Prentice Hall).

The Collected Works of
Langston Hughes

Volume 3

The Poems: 1951–1967

Introduction

By February 1, 1951, the day Langston Hughes celebrated his forty-ninth birthday, he had been publishing poetry for almost thirty consecutive years. In that time he had established himself not only as the poet most beloved among African Americans but also as one of the more admired American poets of his era. The basis of Hughes's reputation was his assiduous devotion to the art of poetry as well as the intensity of his commitment to the depiction of black American culture and to the cause of social justice for all.

As a poet, Hughes had demonstrated time and again a flexibility of temperament and technique that allowed him to establish a solid reputation as a lyric poet of unusual charm and, at the same time, as a highly effective social and political poet. His range stretched from earnest depictions of aspects of nature and loneliness to the most radical expressions of outrage against the inhumanities of racism and unbridled capitalism. His tender awareness of traditional poetic subjects such as nature, love, and loneliness was both offset and fortified in his art by a passionate concern for the welfare of black Americans and poor and oppressed people around the world.

Since the appearance in 1921 of his first poem published in a national journal ("The Negro Speaks of Rivers" in W. E. B. Du Bois's *Crisis* magazine), Hughes had worked hard to maintain his identity as a poet. He had done so in the face of often harsh personal troubles, the indifference or disdain of some publishers, and the occasionally bitter criticism of reviewers, black and white. In the 1920s, the heyday of the Harlem Renaissance, in which he had been one of its brightest stars, Hughes had published his first collection of verse, *The Weary Blues* (Knopf, 1926). The following year, he confirmed his growing mastery of poetic form with *Fine Clothes to the Jew* (Knopf). These volumes illustrated definitively certain conditions of his aesthetic. The most important feature perhaps was his desire to fuse traditional poetic forms, derived from classic Anglo-American literature in particular, with the genius of black expressive culture as represented especially in black speech and music. In this way, Hughes had aligned himself with the great native river of American verse that derived in a real sense from Walt Whitman and his *Leaves of Grass,* which had emphasized as never before the glory of the American language as an expression of the nation's finest character and ideals. Moreover, with *Fine Clothes to the Jew,* Hughes had introduced a new form, the blues, into poetry written in English. For the rest of his life he would continue to rely on this form for inspiration.

The 1930s had been a particularly hard time for Hughes, as it had been for the American people in general. The Great Depression gutted the promise of the Harlem Renaissance and threw into grave doubt the decision of the thousands of blacks who had migrated out of the South into the major cities of the North in search of freedom and prosperity. In response, Hughes had moved politically to the far left, to which he had always been sympathetic. Although he never became a member of the Communist Party, he had lived in the Soviet Union for a year (1932–1933) and in that time had composed some of the most aggressively radical verse ever published by an American writer. Poems such as "Good Morning Revolution" and "Goodbye Christ" bitterly attacked traditional attitudes to government and religion and exhorted the masses to join hands in transforming the world.

The entry of the United States into World War II, as well as severe attacks on Hughes by elements of the religious right because of poems such as "Goodbye Christ," pushed him toward the political center by 1941. Openly repudiating this poem as a relic of his impetuous youth, he threw himself into supporting the war effort. He also began to retool his poetry. *Shakespeare in Harlem* (1942) virtually reintroduced the blues into Hughes's verse. However, his next collection, *Jim Crow's Last Stand* (1943), indicated that Hughes's political zeal was by no means lost. Instead, he was diverting it into vigorous support of the burgeoning civil rights movement in the South led especially by the courageous lawyers of the NAACP.

Later in the decade had come *Fields of Wonder* (1947). Hughes offered this volume as his first entirely lyrical book of verse, by which he probably meant that its major emphasis, despite the presence of other themes, is not on race and politics but on nature. A year later, *One-Way Ticket* took him back to more familiar territory, to a mixture of blues and protest. However, despite his claims about *Fields of Wonder* and his equal pride in *One-Way Ticket,* neither volume broke any new ground in Hughes's evolution as a writer. To a great extent, he was marking time as a poet. In addition, the appearance of these volumes coincided with his growing concern about money, the pursuit of which he had sacrificed in favor of a life of writing. Until 1947, Hughes had saved no money, had accumulated at times significant debt, and had depended in tough times on the charity of patrons and friends. Now, in his middle age, he saw his financial situation as something of a crisis. From this point on, he would pay closer attention to his financial situation. Although his contracts would almost always involve relatively small sums of money, and he even joked about himself as a "literary sharecropper," he would take on more writing tasks than ever before in order to assure himself a decent income as he grew older.[1]

A financial windfall came in 1947 when his role as lyricist with Elmer Rice and Kurt Weill on the successful Broadway musical play *Street Scene* resulted in royalties such as he had never before received. Immediately Hughes set about buying a townhouse at 20 East 127th Street in the heart of Harlem, into which he moved in 1948 with Toy and Emerson Harper, old friends of his mother who had always taken a loving, parental interest in him. Moving into his first home, and one in his beloved Harlem, appeared to set off in him a cloudburst of inspiration. The result was a major book of verse, *Montage of a Dream Deferred.* In September 1948, Hughes breathlessly informed his best friend, Arna Bontemps, about his breakthrough. "I have completed a new book I wrote last week!" Hughes boasted. "No kidding—a full book-length poem in five sections

1. Langston Hughes to Arna Bontemps, August 17, 1952, Langston Hughes Papers, Beinecke Rare Book and Manuscript Library, Yale University.

called *Montage of a Dream Deferred*. Want to see it?" The new poem, he added, "is what you might call a precedent shattering opus—also could be known as a *tour de force*."[2]

Once again, the core element of Hughes's creativity was his attention to black music. In this latest case, that music was bebop. In the iconoclastic music of jazz artists such as Dizzie Gillespie and Charlie Parker, Hughes heard a prophetic commentary on the state of African American reality. The music seemed to announce, in its coded way, the tragic, sometimes manic, collapse of the optimism of the black migration, the Harlem Renaissance, and virtually all other expressions of faith by blacks in the American Dream. Now, with growing unemployment, rising crime, the advent of a drug culture, and a deepening sense of hopelessness, the older Harlem seemed dead. In its place was a new, harshly modern, sometimes neurotic and violent culture struggling nevertheless to uphold old values that emphasized faith and joy. Hughes summed up the relationship between the new music and black people in Harlem in a brief preface to the volume. "This poem on contemporary Harlem," he declared of *Montage of a Dream Deferred,* "is marked by conflicting changes, sudden nuances, sharp and impudent interjections, broken rhythms, and passages sometimes in the manner of the jam session, sometimes the popular song, punctuated by the riffs, runs, breaks, and disc-tortions of the music of a community in transition."

The first piece in the volume sets the tone:

> Good morning, daddy!
> Ain't you heard
> The boogie-woogie rumble
> Of a dream deferred?
>
> Listen closely:
> You'll hear their feet
> Beating out and beating out a—

2. Langston Hughes to Arna Bontemps, September 14, 1948, Langston Hughes Papers, Yale.

> *You think*
> *It's a happy beat?*

> Listen to it closely . . .

This jazz rhythm drives the entire volume but interplays throughout with other rhythms, some of them quite traditional. After all, Harlem residents were by no means devoted to jazz and dance. Some were faithful churchgoers, some were dedicated students, some were mere social strivers, some were people who barely survived. Hughes sought to catch the mood or moods of them all. The most celebrated single poem to emerge from the volume is unquestionably "Harlem." Its quiet, even timid introductory question ("What happens to a dream deferred?") is answered at first patiently and almost resignedly—until out of its reticent heart erupts at last the threat of resistance, violence, and revenge: "*Or does it explode?*"

In between the extremes of boogie-woogie rumble and the threat of explosion are poems that try to do justice to the range of Harlem life. "Theme for English B," for example, also much anthologized, is the meditation of a young man from the South attending a college very much like the City College of New York, not far from Hughes's home. "The instructor said, / *Go home and write / a page tonight*"; and the young man ponders the dilemma he faces as a black student with a white teacher for whom he feels respect and perhaps even affection, but from whom he may be alienated because of the weight of history. "Ballad of the Landlord" ("Landlord, landlord / My roof has sprung a leak") is a mordantly humorous commentary on the sometimes desperate situation concerning housing in Harlem. "Movies" ("The Roosevelt, Renaissance, Gem, Alhambra, / Harlem laughing in all the wrong places / at the crocodile tears / of crocodile art") captures the chasm between white and black values in the most seductive of the media. "Cafe: 3 A.M." ("Detectives from the vice squad / with weary sadistic eyes / spotting fairies") snares an acute image of sexual desire and sexual and perhaps political repression in Harlem. "Brothers" ("We're related—you and I"), recovered for this volume by Hughes from his writings of the 1920s, concisely echoes both the tension and the potential for unity that exist in Harlem as a meeting place for diverse elements of the African Diaspora.

As a volume, *Montage of a Dream Deferred* hardly realized the hopes Hughes had for it in the excitement of its creation. His old publisher, Knopf, saw little promise in the volume and declined to publish it. When the volume appeared (from Henry Holt), reviewers black and white seemed to agree with Knopf. "His images are again quick, vibrant and probing," the distinguished black academic critic J. Saunders Redding wrote, "but they no longer educate. They probe into old emotions and experiences with fine sensitiveness . . . but they reveal nothing new." Another black reviewer reported only "a mélange of self-pity, grief and defeatism." In the *New York Times Book Review,* the respected writer Babette Deutsch derided "a facile sentimentality that stifles real feeling as with cheap scent."[3]

Although abashed by these reviews, Hughes did not stop writing poetry (or believing in the value of his book). He continued to serve the cause of poetry in any useful way he could. That fall, for example, the *Beloit Poetry Chapbook* published his translations of fifteen of the original eighteen ballads in *Romancero Gitano,* or *Gypsy Ballads,* by the celebrated Spanish poet and political martyr Federico García Lorca. In this task, which Hughes saw as a labor of love, the Spanish poet's brother Francisco García Lorca, a professor of literature at Columbia University, aided Hughes. (Hughes also translated García Lorca's play *Bodas de Sangre,* or *Blood Wedding*). In 1957, Indiana University Press published *Selected Poems of Gabriela Mistral,* his translations of verse by the Chilean-born winner of the Nobel Prize for literature Lucila Godoy y Alcayaga. (Hughes had a third volume of translations of verse to his credit. In 1948, the firm of Anderson and Ritchie had brought out his and Ben Frederic Carruthers's *Cuba Libre: Poems by Nicolás Guillén.*) Anthologies were also a significant part of Hughes's service to poetry. In 1949 had come perhaps his most important, coedited with Arna Bontemps: *Poetry of the Negro: 1746–1949* (Doubleday); but before his death he would also

3. *New York Herald Tribune,* March 11, 1951; *Pittsburgh Courier,* March 10, 1951; *New York Times Book Review,* May 6, 1951.

compile collections of the work of younger black American poets as well as of African writers.

After the chilly reception of *Montage of a Dream Deferred,* Hughes did not publish another volume of original verse until a decade had passed. In 1959, Knopf brought out his *Selected Poems.* Setting aside chronology, he had artfully gathered the chosen poems into thematic clusters. However, the book ignored one aspect of his output. Not a single poem indicated that Hughes had once been a firebrand poet of radical socialism. Nevertheless, removing the fangs from his verse did not save *Selected Poems* from criticism. Perhaps the most crushing review came in the *New York Times Book Review* from the rising star of African American literature, the young novelist and essayist James Baldwin. "Every time I read Langston Hughes," Baldwin wrote, "I am amazed all over again by his genuine gifts—and depressed that he has done so little with them."[4]

Baldwin's bizarre review (which he would later repudiate in praising the ways in which Hughes's verse had illuminated Harlem for him as a youth) perhaps had less to do with just criticism than with generational tensions among black writers. Hughes's response, as with earlier criticism, was to watch and wait for major inspiration, even as he continued to write verse. That inspiration came only a year after Baldwin's review, in 1960. Hughes was in Newport, Rhode Island, attending the popular Newport Jazz Festival, when a riot broke out among the fans. Unable to gain admission to the sold-out open-air event and stirred by the music, a crowd of young men stormed the gate and overran the meager police presence there. Police reinforcements fired tear gas and water hoses; the youths responded with bottles and rocks. Eventually, three companies of the National Guard were needed to quell the disturbance. Almost two hundred persons went to jail, and about fifty more were hospitalized with various injuries. The irony of a riot by whites demanding admission to a jazz concert in a city famous for its wealth and style was not lost on Hughes. In the middle of the latest, perhaps climactic phase of the civil rights movement in the South, the rebellion against authority had

4. *New York Times Book Review,* March 29, 1959.

begun to swing to the North and to include younger whites opposed to the old ways. The ancient evils of slavery and Jim Crow were about to be exorcised on a national scale.

On July 4, just after the festival ended, Hughes began to write perhaps the most ambitious single poem of his life. Although he called *Montage of a Dream Deferred,* not without justification, a single poem made up of different parts, what he attempted now was something far more unitary and yet more volatile in its structure. Comprising twelve parts, *Ask Your Mama: 12 Moods for Jazz* was easily the longest single piece of verse that he had ever attempted—and the most experimental. Here the disruptions and discordance that had informed *Montage of a Dream Deferred* are given far wider scope, and quasi-modernistic literary devices such as stream of consciousness, arcane allusiveness, inventive wordplay, "scholarly" notes, and the like are indulged in sharply parodic form by Hughes, within a distinctly African American provenance. The poem begins:

> IN THE
> IN THE QUARTER
> IN THE QUARTER OF THE NEGROES
> WHERE THE DOORS ARE DOORS OF PAPER
> DUST OF DINGY ATOMS
> BLOWS A SCRATCHY SOUND.
> AMORPHOUS JACK-O'-LANTERNS CAPER
> AND THE WIND WON'T WAIT FOR MIDNIGHT
> FOR FUN TO BLOW DOORS DOWN.
>
> BY THE RIVER AND THE RAILROAD
> WITH FLUID FAR-OFF GOING
> BOUNDARIES BIND UNBINDING
> A WHIRL OF WHISTLES BLOWING
> NO TRAINS OR STEAMBOATS GOING—
> YET LEONTYNE'S UNPACKING.
>
> IN THE QUARTER OF THE NEGROES
> WHERE THE DOORKNOBS LET IN LIEDER
> MORE THAN GERMAN EVER BORE,

HER YESTERDAY PAST GRANDPA—
NOT OF HER OWN DOING—
IN A POT OF COLLARD GREENS
IS GENTLY STEWING . . .

As with all of Hughes's best poetry, music is central here. The poem, which comes with musical directions indicated in its margins, invokes not only the American sounds of jazz and the blues but also music from Germany, the Caribbean, Latin America, Africa, and the Jewish liturgical tradition. In addition, it features a distinct African American cultural form, the "Dozens," as perhaps its most influential expressive principle apart from music. The term *Dozens* refers to the game, popular among many younger black Americans, of insults exchanged in a cruelly personal and yet ritualistic competition, usually involving bystanders. Hughes was well aware of the existence of a scholarly article on the subject by the distinguished Yale psychologist John Dollard, "The Dozens: Dialectic of Insult" (1936). In a way that apotheosized elements present both in the Dozens and, in more latent forms, in Hughes's poetry from its beginning, *Ask Your Mama* encoded and transmitted messages of frustration and celebration, parody and rage, humor and solemnity never before vented so intensely in his work.

For all his pains, however, *Ask Your Mama,* published in 1961 in an imaginatively colorful edition by Knopf, fared poorly. The early *Library Journal* appraisal called it "as thin and topical as much of the beat material it resembles," and the *New York Times Book Review* saw only "stunt poetry, a nightclub turn." A few critics wrote of a substantial achievement, and one notable jazz writer, Rudy Blesh, hailed the volume as "the retort—half-derisive, half-angry—to the smug, the stupid, the bigoted, the selfish, the cruel, and the blind among us. . . . With this great theme, a talented poet finds a universal voice."[5] Nevertheless, the book was a clear failure with the majority of readers.

5. *Library Journal,* December 1, 1961; *New York Times Book Review,* October 29, 1961; *New York Herald Tribune,* November 26, 1961.

Ask Your Mama: 12 Moods for Jazz was the last volume published by Hughes in his lifetime. With his literary activity spread more broadly than ever, he seemed to concentrate his poetic talent into the composition of gospel plays such as the popular *Black Nativity*, which includes tender if largely unoriginal lyrics about the birth of Christ, and *The Gospel Glory: A Passion Play*, about the Crucifixion. He also saw himself increasingly at odds with the best known African American poets of his day. This was especially so as the civil rights movement gave way stridently in 1965 to Black Power and to the Black Arts movement led by LeRoi Jones, later Amiri Baraka. Among the more conservative writers, Hughes admired the poetry of Robert Hayden but quietly disapproved of Hayden's efforts to distance himself publicly from the Black Power movement. On the other hand, Hughes detested the foul language and the repressive threats that often emanated from the Black Arts movement. Seen widely by now as virtually the dean of African American poetry, Hughes reacted uneasily to the new movement but did not seek to resign his deanship. In 1964, for example, he was proud to edit *New Negro Poets: U.S.A.* (Indiana University Press).

On the margin as a poet or not, in the last months of his life Hughes began preparing his own poetic tract for the times, a collection of his verse old and new but appropriate to the violent age. This volume, *The Panther and the Lash*, appeared from Knopf not long after Hughes's death in May 1967. The title alludes without doubt to the founding of the Black Panther Party in Oakland, California, the previous year, and its emphasis on black militancy. A part of Hughes was decidedly with the militants, but he had heard the call to revolution at least once before in his life and now saw mainly its limitations. The poem "Black Panther" speaks of "The Panther in his desperate boldness" who has repudiated pacifism ("I don't want to study war no more") and embraced violence ("Eye for eye"); but this Panther, for all his reckless courage, is a man "Motivated by the truest / Of the oldest / Lies." The power of "Final Call" attests to Hughes's urgent and yet quizzical and ironical sense of the apocalypse at hand, the day of final reckoning—perhaps—for the racial sins of American society, from which no one will escape unscathed:

. . . SEND FOR LAFAYETTE AND TELL HIM, "HELP! HELP
   ME!"
SEND FOR DENMARK VESEY CRYING, "FREE!"
FOR CINQUE SAYING, "RUN A NEW FLAG UP THE MAST."
FOR OLD JOHN BROWN WHO KNEW SLAVERY COULDN'T
   LAST.
SEND FOR LENIN! (DON'T YOU DARE!—HE CAN'T COME
   HERE!)
. . . .
DuBOIS (WHEN?) MALCOLM (OH!) SEND FOR STOKELY.
   (NO?) THEN
SEND FOR ADAM POWELL ON A NON-SUBPOENA DAY.
SEND FOR THE PIED PIPER TO PIPE OUR RATS AWAY.

   (And if nobody comes, send for me.)

On the whole, Hughes, once a courageous revolutionary, deliberately kept his distance from the major scenes and events of the 1960s that involved politics and protest. "Politics can be the graveyard of the poet," he wrote privately in 1964. "And only poetry can be his resurrection." Thus to the end he arbitrated between his desire to be a poet and his desire to move society on the question of social justice. This was the central tension of Langston Hughes's life as a writer. In the 1930s, under desperate circumstances, he had lost his way as a poet and given himself to political dogma and propaganda. Now, at the end, feeling the tide of American history sweeping by, he remained true to his art, which could never be severed from the lives and fate of black Americans.

"Hang yourself, poet, in your own words," he had gone on to insist in that meditation of 1964. "Otherwise you are dead."[6] His poetry was indeed a continuous act of courage as well as a continuous act of art. Hughes was among the bravest and best of our American poets, and the legacy of his verse will continue to challenge, beguile, and inspire readers for many generations to come.

6. Langston Hughes, "Draft ideas," ms., December 3, 1964.

A Note on the Text

In presenting this three-volume edition of the poems of Langston Hughes as part of our *Collected Works of Langston Hughes,* we have chosen to highlight the individual books of verse prepared and published by Hughes, as opposed to a presentation of each poem in strict chronological order according to the date of its first publication, as in *The Collected Poems of Langston Hughes,* edited by Arnold Rampersad and David Roessel (New York: Knopf, 1994).

Thus, in Volume 3 (1951–1967) we offer the texts of three complete books of poems—*Montage of a Dream Deferred* (1951), *Ask Your Mama* (1961), and *The Panther and the Lash* (1967). In those few instances in which Hughes published the same poem (or an altered version) in two different volumes, we have included both printings of the poem in order to preserve the harmony of each volume. We have chosen not to republish Hughes's own *Selected Poems* (1959), which contained no new material. In the case of *Montage of a Dream Deferred,* as elsewhere, we have preserved the exact text of the first edition despite changes later made by Hughes in his *Langston Hughes Reader* (George Braziller) and *Selected Poems* (Knopf).

"Uncollected" poems from 1951 to 1967, if they did not appear in a later book of verse prepared by Hughes, are presented in chronological order according to the date of their first publication. The texts of these "uncollected" poems come in general from Rampersad and Roessel, eds., *Collected Poems of Langston Hughes.* This volume, which presents the *last* published version of each poem, should be consulted for its bibliographical notes and other information.

Montage of a Dream Deferred

(1951)

To Ralph and Fanny Ellison

I am grateful to the editors of *Holiday, Tomorrow, Our World, Common Ground, The Midwest Journal, The Crisis, Phylon, Voices,* and *The Harlem Quarterly* for permission to reprint the sections of this poem which first appeared in their pages.

In terms of current Afro-American popular music and the sources from which it has progressed—jazz, ragtime, swing, blues, boogie-woogie, and be-bop—this poem on contemporary Harlem, like be-bop, is marked by conflicting changes, sudden nuances, sharp and impudent interjections, broken rhythms, and passages sometimes in the manner of the jam session, sometimes the popular song, punctuated by the riffs, runs, breaks, and disc-tortions of the music of a community in transition.

Contents

Early Bright

Lenox Avenue Mural

Boogie Segue to Bop

Dream Boogie

Good morning, daddy!
Ain't you heard
The boogie-woogie rumble
Of a dream deferred?

Listen closely:
You'll hear their feet
Beating out and beating out a—

   You think
   It's a happy beat?

Listen to it closely:
Ain't you heard
something underneath
like a—

   What did I say?

Sure,
I'm happy!
Take it away!

   Hey, pop!
   Re-bop!
   Mop!

   Y-e-a-h!

Parade

Seven ladies
and seventeen gentlemen
at the Elks Club Lounge
planning planning a parade:
Grand Marshal in his white suit
will lead it.
Cadillacs with dignitaries
will precede it.
And behind will come
with band and drum
on foot . . . on foot . . .
on foot . . .

Motorcycle cops,
white,
will speed it
out of sight
if they can:
Solid black,
can't be right.

Marching . . . marching . . .
marching . . .
noon till night . . .

 I never knew
 that many Negroes
 were on earth,
 did you?

 I never knew!

  PARADE!

 A chance to let

PARADE!

the whole world see

PARADE!

old black me!

Children's Rhymes

When I was a chile we used to play,
"One—two—buckle my shoe!"
and things like that. But now, Lord,
listen at them little varmints!

By what sends
the white kids
I ain't sent:
I know I can't
be President.

There is two thousand children
in this block, I do believe!

What don't bug
them white kids
sure bugs me:
We knows everybody
ain't free!

Some of these young ones is cert'ly bad—
One batted a hard ball right through my window
and my gold fish et the glass.

What's written down
for white folks

ain't for us a-tall:
"Liberty And Justice—
Huh—For All."

Oop-pop-a-da!
Skee! Daddle-de-do!
Be-bop!

Salt'peanuts!

De-dop!

Sister

That little Negro's married and got a kid.
Why does he keep on foolin' around Marie?
Marie's my sister—not married to me—
But why does *he* keep on foolin' around Marie?
Why don't she get a boy-friend
I can understand—some decent man?

> *Did it ever occur to you, son,*
> *the reason Marie runs around with trash*
> *is she wants some cash?*

Don't decent folks have dough?

> *Unfortunately usually no!*

Well, anyway, it don't have to be a married man.

> *Did it ever occur to you, boy,*
> *that a woman does the best she can?*

Comment on Stoop

So does a man.

Preference

I likes a woman
six or eight and ten years older'n myself.
I don't fool with these young girls.
Young girl'll say,
   Daddy, I want so-and-so.
   I needs this, that, and the other.
But a old woman'll say,
   Honey, what does YOU need?
   I just drawed my money tonight
   and it's all your'n.
That's why I likes a older woman
who can appreciate me:
When she conversations you
it ain't forever, *Gimme*!

Necessity

Work?
I don't have to work.
I don't have to do nothing
but eat, drink, stay black, and die.
This little old furnished room's
so small I can't whip a cat
without getting fur in my mouth
and my landlady's so old
her features is all run together
and God knows she sure can overcharge—

Which is why I reckon I *does*
have to work after all.

Question

Said the lady, *Can you do*
what my other man can't do—
That is
love me, daddy—
and feed me, too?

Figurine

De-dop!

Buddy

That kid's my buddy,
still and yet
I don't see him much.
He works downtown for Twelve a week.
Has to give his mother Ten—
she says he can have
the other Two
to pay his carfare, buy a suit,
coat, shoes,
anything he wants out of it.

Juke Box Love Song

I could take the Harlem night
and wrap around you,
Take the neon lights and make a crown,
Take the Lenox Avenue busses,
Taxis, subways,
And for your love song tone their rumble down.
Take Harlem's heartbeat,
Make a drumbeat,
Put it on a record, let it whirl,
And while we listen to it play,
Dance with you till day—
Dance with you, my sweet brown Harlem girl.

Ultimatum

Baby, how come you can't see me
when I'm paying your bills
each and every week?

If you got somebody else,
tell me—
else I'll cut you off
without your rent.
I mean
without a cent.

Warning

Daddy,
don't let your dog
curb you!

Croon

I don't give a damn
For Alabam'
Even if it is my home.

New Yorkers

I was born here,
that's no lie, he said,
right here beneath God's sky.

> *I wasn't born here, she said,*
> *I come—and why?*
> *Where I come from*
> *folks work hard*
> *all their lives*
> *until they die*
> *and never own no parts*
> *of earth nor sky.*
> *So I come up here.*
> *Now what've I got?*
> *You!*

She lifted up her lips
in the dark:
The same old spark!

Wonder

Early blue evening.
Lights ain't come on yet.
Looky yonder!
They come on now!

Easy Boogie

Down in the bass
That steady beat
Walking walking walking
Like marching feet.

Down in the bass
That easy roll,
Rolling like I like it
In my soul.

   Riffs, smears, breaks.

Hey, Lawdy, Mama!
Do you hear what I said?
Easy like I rock it
In my bed!

Dig and Be Dug

Movies

The Roosevelt, Renaissance, Gem, Alhambra:
Harlem laughing in all the wrong places
   at the crocodile tears
   of crocodile art
   that you know
   in your heart
   is crocodile:

     (Hollywood
        laughs at me,
        black—
        so I laugh
        back.)

Tell Me

Why should it be *my* loneliness,
Why should it be *my* song,
Why should it be *my* dream
   deferred
   overlong?

Not a Movie

Well, they rocked him with road-apples
because he tried to vote
and whipped his head with clubs

and he crawled on his knees to his house
and he got the midnight train
and he crossed that Dixie line
now he's livin'
on a 133rd.

He didn't stop in Washington
and he didn't stop in Baltimore
neither in Newark on the way.
Six knots was on his head
but, thank God, he wasn't dead,
now there ain't no Ku Klux
on a 133rd.

Neon Signs

WONDER BAR
∴
WISHING WELL
∴
MONTEREY
∴
MINTON'S
(altar of Thelonious)
∴
MANDALAY
∴
Spots where the booted
and unbooted play
∴
LENOX
∴
CASBAH
∴

POOR JOHN'S
∴

Mirror-go-round
where a broken glass
in the early bright
smears re-bop
sound

Numbers

If I ever hit for a dollar
gonna salt every dime away
in the Post Office for a rainy day.

I ain't gonna
play back a cent.

(Of course, I might
combinate *a little*
with my rent.)

What? So Soon!

I believe my old lady's
pregnant again!

Fate must have
some kind of trickeration
to populate the
cullud nation!

Comment against Lamp Post

You call it fate?

Figurette

De-daddle-dy!
De-dop!

Motto

I play it cool
And dig all jive
That's the reason
I stay alive.

My motto,
As I live and learn,
    is:
Dig And Be Dug
In Return.

Dead in There

Sometimes
A night funeral
Going by
Carries home
A re-bop daddy.

Hearse and flowers
Guarantee

He'll never hype
Another paddy.

It's hard to believe,
But dead in there,
He'll never lay a
Hype nowhere!

He's my ace-boy,
Gone away.
Wake up and live!
He used to say.

Squares
Who couldn't dig him,
Plant him now—
Out where it makes
No diff' no how.

Situation

When I rolled three 7's
in a row
I was scared to walk out
with the dough.

Dancer

Two or three things in the past
failed him
that had not failed people
of lesser genius.

In the first place
he didn't have much sense.
He was no good at making love
and no good at making money.
So he tapped,
   trucked,
   boogied,
   sanded,
   jittered,
until he made folks say,
   Looky yonder
   at that boy!
   Hey!

But being no good at lovin'—
the girls left him.
(When you're no good for dough they go.)
With no sense, just wonderful feet,
What could possibly be all-reet?
Did he get anywhere? No!

Even a great dancer
can't C.P.T.
a show.

Advice

Folks, I'm telling you,
birthing is hard
and dying is mean—
so get yourself
a little loving
in between.

Green Memory

A wonderful time—the War:
when money rolled in
and blood rolled out.

But blood
was far away
from here—

Money was near.

Wine-O

Setting in the wine-house
Soaking up a wine-souse
Waiting for tomorrow to come—
Then
Setting in the wine-house
Soaking up a new souse.
Tomorrow . . . .
Oh, hum!

Relief

My heart is aching
for them Poles and Greeks
on relief way across the sea
because I was on relief
once in 1933.

I know what relief can be—
it took me two years to get on W.P.A.
If the war hadn't come along

I wouldn't be out of the barrel yet.
Now, I'm almost back in the barrel again.

To tell the truth,
if these white folks want to go ahead
and fight another war,
or even two,
the one to stop 'em won't be me.

Would you?

Ballad of the Landlord

Landlord, landlord,
My roof has sprung a leak.
Don't you 'member I told you about it
Way last week?

Landlord, landlord,
These steps is broken down.
When you come up yourself
It's a wonder you don't fall down.

Ten Bucks you say I owe you?
Ten Bucks you say is due?
Well, that's Ten Bucks more'n I'll pay you
Till you fix this house up new.

What? You gonna get eviction orders?
You gonna cut off my heat?
You gonna take my furniture and
Throw it in the street?

Um-huh! You talking high and mighty.
Talk on—till you get through.

You ain't gonna be able to say a word
If I land my fist on you.

Police! Police!
Come and get this man!
He's trying to ruin the government
And overturn the land!

Copper's whistle!
Patrol bell!
Arrest.

Precinct Station.
Iron cell.
Headlines in press:

MAN THREATENS LANDLORD

∴

TENANT HELD NO BAIL

∴

JUDGE GIVES NEGRO 90 DAYS IN COUNTY JAIL

Corner Meeting

Ladder, flag, and amplifier:
what the soap box
used to be.

The speaker catches fire
looking at their faces.

His words
jump down to stand
in listeners' places.

Projection

On the day when the Savoy
leaps clean over to Seventh Avenue
and starts jitterbugging
with the Renaissance,
on that day when Abyssinia Baptist Church
throws her enormous arms around
St. James Presbyterian
and 409 Edgecombe
stoops to kiss 12 West 133rd,
on that day—
Do, Jesus!
Manhattan Island will whirl
like a Dizzy Gillespie transcription
played by Inez and Timme.
On that day, Lord,
Willie Bryant and Marian Anderson
will sing a duet,
Paul Robeson
will team up with Jackie Mabley,
and Father Divine will say in truth,
   Peace!
   It's truly
   wonderful!

Early Bright

Flatted Fifths

Little cullud boys with beards
re-bop be-bop mop and stop.

Little cullud boys with fears,
frantic, kick their CC years
into flatted fifths and flatter beers
that at a sudden change become
sparkling Oriental wines
rich and strange
silken bathrobes with gold twines
and Heilbroner, Crawford,
Nat-undreamed-of Lewis combines
in silver thread and diamond notes
on trade-marks inside
Howard coats.

Little cullud boys in berets
   oop pop-a-da
horse a fantasy of days
   ool ya koo
and dig all plays.

Tomorrow

Tomorrow may be
a thousand years off:

TWO DIMES AND A NICKEL ONLY

says this particular
cigarette machine.

Others take a quarter straight.

Some dawns
wait.

Mellow

Into the laps
of black celebrities
white girls fall
like pale plums from a tree
beyond a high tension wall
wired for killing
which makes it
more thrilling.

Live and Let Live

Maybe it ain't right—
but the people of the night
    will give even
    a snake
    a break.

Gauge

Hemp . . . .
A stick . . . .
A roach . . . .
Straw . . . .

Bar

That whisky will cook the egg.

> *Say not so!*
> *Maybe the egg*
> *will cook the whisky.*

You ought to know!

Cafe: 3 A.M.

Detectives from the vice squad
with weary sadistic eyes
spotting fairies.

> *Degenerates,*
> some folks say.

> But God, Nature,
> or somebody
> made them that way.

Police lady or Lesbian
over there?

> *Where?*

Drunkard

Voice grows thicker
as song grows stronger
as time grows longer until day
trying to forget to remember
the taste of day.

Street Song

Jack, if you got to be a rounder
Be a rounder right—
Just don't let mama catch you
Makin' rounds at night.

125th Street

Face like a chocolate bar
full of nuts and sweet.

Face like a jack-o'-lantern,
candle inside.

Face like slice of melon,
grin that wide.

Dive

Lenox Avenue
by daylight
runs to dive in the Park
but faster . . .

faster . . .
after dark.

Warning: Augmented

Don't let your dog curb you!
   Curb your doggie
   Like you ought to do,
But don't let that dog curb you!
   You may play folks cheap,
   Act rough and tough,
   But a dog can tell
   When you're full of stuff.
Don't let your dog curb you!
   Watch your step—
   Else before you're through
You're liable to find your dog's curbed you!
   Them little old mutts
   Look all scraggly and bad,
   But they got more sense
   Than some hustlers ever had.
Cur dog, fice dog, keary blue—
Just don't let your dog curb you!

Up-Beat

In the gutter
boys who try
might meet girls
on the fly
as out of the gutter
girls who will
may meet boys
copping a thrill

while from the gutter
both can rise:
But it requires
plenty eyes.

Jam Session

Letting midnight
out on bail
  pop-a-da
having been
detained in jail
  oop-pop-a-da
for sprinkling salt
on a dreamer's tail
  pop-a-da

Be-Bop Boys

Imploring Mecca
to achieve
six discs
with Decca.

Tag

Little cullud boys
  with fears,
  frantic,
nudge their draftee years.

  Pop-a-da!

Vice Versa to Bach

Theme for English B

The instructor said,

> *Go home and write*
> *a page tonight.*
> *And let that page come out of you—*
> *Then, it will be true.*

I wonder if it's that simple?
I am twenty-two, colored, born in Winston-Salem.
I went to school there, then Durham, then here
to this college on the hill above Harlem.
I am the only colored student in my class.
The steps from the hill lead down into Harlem,
through a park, then I cross St. Nicholas,
Eighth Avenue, Seventh, and I come to the Y,
the Harlem Branch Y, where I take the elevator
up to my room, sit down, and write this page:

It's not easy to know what is true for you or me
at twenty-two, my age. But I guess I'm what
I feel and see and hear, Harlem, I hear you:
hear you, hear me—we two—you, me, talk on this page.
(I hear New York, too.) Me—who?
Well, I like to eat, sleep, drink, and be in love.
I like to work, read, learn, and understand life.
I like a pipe for a Christmas present,
or records—Bessie, bop, or Bach.
I guess being colored doesn't make me *not* like
the same things other folks like who are other races.

So will my page be colored that I write?
Being me, it will not be white.
But it will be
a part of you, instructor.
You are white—
yet a part of me, as I am a part of you.
That's American.
Sometimes perhaps you don't want to be a part of me.
Nor do I often want to be a part of you.
But we are, that's true!
As I learn from you,
I guess you learn from me—
although you're older—and white—
and somewhat more free.

This is my page for English B.

College Formal: Renaissance Casino

Golden girl
in a golden gown
in a melody night
in Harlem town
lad tall and brown
tall and wise
college boy smart
eyes in eyes
the music wraps
them both around
in mellow magic
of dancing sound
till they're the heart
of the whole big town
gold and brown

Low to High

How can you forget me?
But you do!
You said you was gonna take me
Up with you—
Now you've got your Cadillac,
you done forgot that you are black.
How can you forget me
When I'm you?

But you do.

How can you forget me,
fellow, say?
How can you low-rate me
this way?
You treat me like you damn well please,
Ignore me—though I pay your fees.
How can you forget me?

But you do.

Boogie: 1 A.M.

Good evening, daddy!
I know you've heard
The boogie-woogie rumble
Of a dream deferred
Trilling the treble
And twining the bass
Into midnight ruffles
Of cat-gut lace.

High to Low

God knows
We have our troubles, too—
One trouble is you:
you talk too loud,
cuss too loud,
look too black,
don't get anywhere,
and sometimes it seems
you don't even care.
The way you send your kids to school
stockings down,
(not Ethical Culture)
the way you shout out loud in church,
(not St. Phillips)
and the way you lounge on doorsteps
just as if you were down South,
(not at 409)
the way you clown—
the way, in other words,
you let me down—
me, trying to uphold the race
and you—
well, you can see,
we have our problems,
too, with you.

Lady's Boogie

See that lady
Dressed so fine?
She ain't got boogie-woogie
On her mind—

But if she was to listen
I bet she'd hear,
Way up in the treble
The tingle of a tear.

Be-Bach!

Freedom Train

I read in the papers about the
    Freedom Train.
I heard on the radio about the
    Freedom Train.
I went down to the station and seen the
    Freedom Train.
Lord, I been a-waitin' for the
    Freedom Train!

Down South in Dixie only train I see's
Got a Jim Crow car set aside for me.
I hope there ain't no Jim Crow on the Freedom Train,
No back door entrance to the Freedom Train,
No signs FOR COLORED on the Freedom Train,
No WHITE FOLKS ONLY on the Freedom Train.

I'm gonna check up on this
    Freedom Train.

Who's the engineer on the Freedom Train?
Can a coal black man drive the Freedom Train?
Or am I still a porter on the Freedom Train?
Is there ballot boxes on the Freedom Train?
Do colored folks vote on the Freedom Train?
When it stops in Mississippi will it be made plain
Everybody's got a right to board the Freedom Train?

Somebody tell me about this
　　Freedom Train!

The Birmingham station's marked COLORED and WHITE.
The white folks go left, the colored go right—
They even got a segregated lane.
Is that the way to get aboard the Freedom Train?

　I got to know about this
　　Freedom Train!

If my children ask me, *Daddy, please explain*
Why there's Jim Crow stations for the Freedom Train,
What shall I tell my children? . . . *You* tell me—
'Cause freedom ain't freedom when a man ain't free.

　But maybe they'll explain it on the
　　Freedom Train.

When my old grandma in Atlanta, 83 and black,
Gets in line to see the Freedom,
Will some white man yell, *Get back!*
A Negra's got no business on the Freedom Track!

　But, Mister, I thought it were the
　　Freedom Train!

One grandson's name was Jimmy. He died at Anzio.
He died for real. It warn't no show.
The freedom that they carryin' on this Freedom Train,
Is it for real—or just a show again?

　Jimmy wants to know about this
　　Freedom Train.

Will *his* Freedom Train come zoomin' down the track
Gleamin' in the sunlight for white and black?
Not stoppin' at no stations marked COLORED and WHITE,

Just stoppin' in the fields in the broad daylight,
Stoppin' in the country in the wide open air
Where there never was no Jim Crow signs nowhere,
No Welcomin' Committees, nor politicians of note,
No lily-white Mayors for which colored can't vote,
And nary a sign of a color line—
For the Freedom Train will be yours and mine!

Then maybe from their graves in Anzio
The G.I.'s who fought will say,
    We wanted it so!
Black men and white will say,
    Ain't it fine?
    At home we got a train
    That's yours and mine!

    Then I'll shout,
    Glory for the
    Freedom Train!

    I'll holler,
    Blow your whistle,
    Freedom Train!

    Thank-God-A-Mighty!
    Here's the
    Freedom Train!

Get on board our Freedom Train!

Deferred

This year, maybe, do you think I can graduate?
I'm already two years late.
Dropped out six months when I was seven,

a year when I was eleven,
then got put back when we come North.
To get through high at twenty's kind of late—
But maybe this year I can graduate.

Maybe now I can have that white enamel stove
I dreamed about when we first fell in love
eighteen years ago.
But you know,
rooming and everything
then kids,
cold-water flat and all that.
But now my daughter's married
And my boy's most grown—
quit school to work—
and where we're moving
there ain't no stove—
Maybe I can buy that white enamel stove!

Me, I always did want to study French.
It don't make sense—
I'll never go to France,
but night schools teach French.
Now at last I've got a job
where I get off at five,
in time to wash and dress,
so, s'il-vous plait, *I'll study French!*

Someday,
I'm gonna buy two new suits
at once!

All I want is
one more bottle of gin.

All I want is to see
my furniture paid for.

*All I want is a wife who will
work with me and not against me. Say,
baby, could you see your way clear?*

Heaven, heaven, is my home!
This world I'll leave behind.
When I set my feet in glory
I'll have a throne for mine!

I want to pass the civil service.

I want a television set.

*You know, as old as I am,
I ain't never
owned a decent radio yet?*

I'd like to take up Bach.

　　*Montage
　　of a dream
　　deferred.*

Buddy, have you heard?

Request

Gimme $25.00
and the change.
I'm going
where the morning
and the evening
won't bother me.

Shame on You

If you're great enough
and clever enough
the government might honor you.
But the people will forget—
Except on holidays.

A movie house in Harlem named after Lincoln,
Nothing at all named after John Brown.

Black people don't remember
any better than white.

If you're not alive and kicking,
shame on you!

World War II

What a grand time was the war!
    Oh, my, my!
What a grand time was the war!
    My, my, my!

In wartime we had fun,
Sorry that old war is done!
What a grand time was the war,
My, my!

Echo:

    Did
    Somebody
    Die?

Dream Deferred

Mystery

When a chile gets to be thirteen
and ain't seen Christ yet,
she needs to set on de moaner's bench
night and day.

Jesus, lover of my soul!

Hail, Mary, mother of God!

Let me to thy bosom fly!

Amen! Hallelujah!

Swing low, sweet chariot,
Coming for to carry me home.

Sunday morning where the rhythm flows,
how old nobody knows—
yet old as mystery,
older than creed,
basic and wondering
and lost as my need.

   Eli, eli!

   Te deum!

   Mahomet!

   Christ!

Father Bishop, Effendi, Mother Horne,
Father Divine, a Rabbi black

as black was born,
a jack-leg preacher, a Ph.D.

> *The mystery*
> *and the darkness*
> *and the song*
> *and me.*

Sliver of Sermon

When pimps out of loneliness cry:
    Great God!
Whores in final weariness say:
    Great God!
Mothers who've lost their last sons weep:
    Great God!
    Oh, God!
    My God!

    Great
    God!

Testimonial

If I just had a piano,
if I just had a organ,
if I just had a drum,
how I could praise my Lord!

But I don't need no piano,
    neither organ
    nor drum
for to praise my Lord!

Passing

On sunny summer Sunday afternoons in Harlem
when the air is one interminable ball game
and grandma cannot get her gospel hymns
from the Saints of God in Christ
on account of the Dodgers on the radio,
on sunny Sunday afternoons
when the kids look all new
and far too clean to stay that way,
and Harlem has its
washed-and-ironed-and-cleaned-best out,
the ones who've crossed the line
to live downtown
miss you,
Harlem of the bitter dream,
since their dream has
come true.

Nightmare Boogie

I had a dream
and I could see
a million faces
black as me!
A nightmare dream:
Quicker than light
All them faces
Turned dead white!
Boogie-woogie,
Rolling bass,
Whirling treble
Of cat-gut lace.

Sunday by the Combination

I feel like dancin', baby,
till the sun goes down.

But I wonder where
the sunrise
Monday morning's gonna be?

I feel like dancin'!
Baby, dance with me!

Casualty

He was a soldier in the army,
But he doesn't walk like one.
He walks like his soldiering
Days are done.

Son! . . . Son!

Night Funeral in Harlem

Night funeral
In Harlem:

*Where did they get
Them two fine cars?*

Insurance man, he did not pay—
His insurance lapsed the other day—
Yet they got a satin box
For his head to lay.

Night funeral
In Harlem:

Who was it sent
That wreath of flowers?

Them flowers came
from that poor boy's friends—
They'll want flowers, too,
When they met their ends.

Night funeral
In Harlem:

Who preached that
Black boy to his grave?

Old preacher-man
Preached that boy away—
Charged Five Dollars
His girl friend had to pay.

Night funeral
In Harlem:

When it was all over
And the lid shut on his head
and the organ had done played
and the last prayers been said
and six pallbearers
Carried him out for dead
And off down Lenox Avenue
That long black hearse done sped,
The street light
At his corner
Shined just like a tear—
That boy that they was mournin'

Was so dear, so dear
To them folks that brought the flowers,
To that girl who paid the preacher-man—
It was all their tears that made
    That poor boy's
    Funeral grand.

    Night funeral
    In Harlem.

Blues at Dawn

I don't dare start thinking in the morning.
I don't dare start thinking in the morning.
    If I thought thoughts in bed,
    Them thoughts would bust my head—
So I don't dare start thinking in the morning.

I don't dare remember in the morning.
Don't dare remember in the morning.
    If I recall the day before,
    I wouldn't get up no more—
So I don't dare remember in the morning.

Dime

Chile, these steps is hard to climb.

    Grandma, lend me a dime.

Montage of a dream deferred:

    Grandma acts like
    She ain't heard.

Chile, Granny ain't got no dime.

I might've knowed
It all the time.

Argument

White is right,
Yellow mellow,
Black, get back!

Do you believe that, Jack?

Sure do!

Then you're a dope
for which there ain't no hope.
Black is fine!
And, God knows,
It's mine!

Neighbor

Down home
he sets on a stoop
and watches the sun go by.
In Harlem
when his work is done
he sets in a bar with a beer.
He looks taller than he is
and younger than he ain't.
He looks darker than he is, too.
And he's smarter than he looks.

He ain't smart.
That cat's a fool.

Naw, he ain't neither.
He's a good man,
except that he talks too much.
In fact, he's a great cat.
But when he drinks,
he drinks fast.

Sometimes
he don't drink.

True,
he just
lets his glass
set there.

Evening Song

A woman standing in the doorway
Trying to make her where-with-all:
Come here, baby, darlin'!
Don't you hear me call?

If I was anybody's sister,
I'd tell her, *Gimme a place to sleep.*
But I ain't nobody's sister.
I'm just a poor lost sheep.

Mary, Mary, Mary,
Had a little lamb.
Well, I hope that lamb of Mary's
Don't turn out like I am.

Chord

Shadow faces
In the shadow night
Before the early dawn
Bops bright.

Fact

There's been an eagle on a nickel,
An eagle on a quarter, too.
But there ain't no eagle
On a dime.

Joe Louis

They worshipped Joe.
A school teacher
whose hair was gray
said:

> *Joe has sense enough to know*
> *He is a god.*
> *So many gods don't know.*

"They say" . . . "They say" . . . "They say" . . .
But the gossips had no
"They say"
to latch onto
for Joe.

Subway Rush Hour

Mingled
breath and smell
so close
mingled
black and white
so near
no room for fear.

Brothers

We're related—you and I,
You from the West Indies,
I from Kentucky.

Kinsmen—you and I,
You from Africa,
I from the U.S.A.

Brothers—you and I—

Likewise

The Jews:
   Groceries
   Suits
   Fruit
   Watches
   Diamond rings
   THE DAILY NEWS
Jews sell me things.
Yom Kippur, no!

Shops all over Harlem
close up tight that night.

Some folks blame high prices on the Jews.
(Some folks blame too much on Jews).
But in Harlem they don't answer back,
Just maybe shrug their shoulders,
"What's the use?"
What's the use
In Harlem?
What's the use?
What's the Harlem
use in Harlem
what's the lick?

Hey!
Baba-re-bop!
Mop.
On a be-bop kick!

Sometimes I think
Jews must have heard
the music of a
dream deferred.

Sliver

Cheap little rhymes,
A cheap little tune
Are sometimes as dangerous
As a sliver of the moon.

A cheap little tune
To cheap little rhymes
Can cut a man's
Throat sometimes.

Hope

He rose up on his dying bed
and asked for fish.
His wife looked it up in her dream book
and played it.

Dream Boogie: Variation

Tinkling treble,
Rolling bass,
High noon teeth
In a midnight face,
Great long fingers
On great big hands,
Screaming pedals
Where his twelve-shoe lands,
Looks like his eyes
Are teasing pain,
A few minutes late
For the Freedom Train.

Lenox Avenue Mural

Harlem

What happens to a dream deferred?

> Does it dry up
> like a raisin in the sun?
> Or fester like a sore—
> And then run?
> Does it stink like rotten meat?
> Or crust and sugar over—
> like a syrupy sweet?

> Maybe it just sags
> like a heavy load.

> *Or does it explode?*

Good Morning

Good morning, daddy!
I was born here, he said,
watched Harlem grow
until colored folks spread
from river to river
across the middle of Manhattan
out of Penn Station
dark tenth of a nation,
planes from Puerto Rico,
and holds of boats, chico,
up from Cuba Haiti Jamaica,

in busses marked NEW YORK
from Georgia Florida Louisiana
to Harlem Brooklyn the Bronx
but most of all to Harlem
dusky sash across Manhattan
I've seen them come dark
   wondering
   wide-eyed
   dreaming
out of Penn Station—
but the trains are late.
The gates open—
    Yet there're bars
    at each gate.

    What happens
    to a dream deferred?

    Daddy, ain't you heard?

Same in Blues

I said to my baby,
Baby, take it slow.
I can't, she said, I can't!
I got to go!

   There's a certain
   amount of traveling
   in a dream deferred.

Lulu said to Leonard,
I want a diamond ring.
Leonard said to Lulu,
You won't get a goddamn thing!

A certain
amount of nothing
in a dream deferred.

Daddy, daddy, daddy,
All I want is you.

Comment on Curb

You talk like
they don't kick
dreams around
Downtown.

> *I expect they do—*
> *But I'm talking about*
> *Harlem to you!*

Letter

Dear Mama,
    Time I pay rent and get my food
and laundry I don't have much left
but here is five dollars for you
to show you I still appreciates you.
My girl-friend send her love and say
she hopes to lay eyes on you sometime in life.
Mama, it has been raining cats and dogs up
here. Well, that is all so I will close.
    Your son baby
        Respectably as ever,
            Joe

Island

Between two rivers,
North of the park,
Like darker rivers
The streets are dark.

Black and white,
Gold and brown—
Chocolate-custard
Pie of a town.

Dream within a dream,
Our dream deferred.

Good morning, daddy!

Ain't you heard?

Ask Your Mama

12 Moods for Jazz

(1961)

Acknowledgment

The author wishes to thank the editors of *Poetry, The Village Voice, Voices, The Crisis,* and *Jazz Today* for permission to reprint those sections of this poem previously published in their pages.

To Louis Armstrong   *the greatest*
horn blower
of them all

Hesitation Blues

(Traditional)

The traditional folk melody of the "Hesitation Blues"
is the leitmotif for this poem. In and around it,
along with the other recognizable melodies employed,
there is room for spontaneous jazz improvisation,
particularly between verses,
where the voice pauses.
The musical figurine indicated after each "Ask your mama"
line may incorporate the impudent little melody of the old break,
"Shave and a haircut, fifteen cents."

Shave and a Haircut

(Figurine)

Contents

Cultural Exchange

IN THE	*The*
IN THE QUARTER	*rhythmically*
IN THE QUARTER OF THE NEGROES	*rough*
WHERE THE DOORS ARE DOORS OF PAPER	*scraping*
DUST OF DINGY ATOMS	*of a guira*
BLOWS A SCRATCHY SOUND.	*continues*
AMORPHOUS JACK-O'-LANTERNS CAPER	*monotonously*
AND THE WIND WON'T WAIT FOR MIDNIGHT	*until a lonely*
FOR FUN TO BLOW DOORS DOWN.	*flute call,*
	high and
BY THE RIVER AND THE RAILROAD	*far away,*
WITH FLUID FAR-OFF GOING	*merges*
BOUNDARIES BIND UNBINDING	*into piano*
A WHIRL OF WHISTLES BLOWING	*variations*
NO TRAINS OR STEAMBOATS GOING—	*on German*
YET LEONTYNE'S UNPACKING.	*lieder*
	gradually
IN THE QUARTER OF THE NEGROES	*changing*
WHERE THE DOORKNOB LETS IN LIEDER	*into*
MORE THAN GERMAN EVER BORE,	*old-time*
HER YESTERDAY PAST GRANDPA—	*traditional*
NOT OF HER OWN DOING—	*12-bar*
IN A POT OF COLLARD GREENS	*blues*
IS GENTLY STEWING.	*up strong*
	between verses
THERE, FORBID US TO REMEMBER,	*until*
COMES AN AFRICAN IN MID-DECEMBER	*African*
SENT BY THE STATE DEPARTMENT	*drums*
AMONG THE SHACKS TO MEET THE BLACKS:	*throb*
LEONTYNE SAMMY HARRY POITIER	*against*

LOVELY LENA MARIAN LOUIS PEARLIE MAE   *blues*

GEORGE S. SCHUYLER MOLTO BENE   *fading*
COME WHAT MAY LANGSTON HUGHES   *as the*
IN THE QUARTER OF THE NEGROES   *music*
WHERE THE RAILROAD AND THE RIVER   *ends.*
HAVE DOORS THAT FACE EACH WAY   TACIT
AND THE ENTRANCE TO THE MOVIE'S
UP AN ALLEY UP THE SIDE.

                                                    "Hesitation
PUSHCARTS FOLD AND UNFOLD   *Blues" with*
IN A SUPERMARKET SEA.   *full band*
AND WE BETTER FIND OUT, MAMA,   *up strong*
WHERE IS THE COLORED LAUNDROMAT,   *for a chorus*
SINCE WE MOVED UP TO MOUNT VERNON.   *in the clear*
                                                    between verses
RALPH ELLISON AS VESPUCIUS   *then down*
INA-YOURA AT THE MASTHEAD   *under voice*
ARNA BONTEMPS CHIEF CONSULTANT   *softly as*
MOLTO BENE MELLOW BABY PEARLIE MAE   *deep-toned*
SHALOM ALEICHEM JIMMY BALDWIN SAMMY   *distant*
COME WHAT MAY—THE SIGNS POINT: *African*
    GHANA   GUINEA   *drums*
AND THE TOLL BRIDGE FROM WESTCHESTER   *join the*
IS A GANGPLANK ROCKING RISKY   *blues until*
BETWEEN THE DECK AND SHORE   *the music*
OF A BOAT THAT NEVER QUITE   *dies. . . .*
KNEW ITS DESTINATION.

IN THE QUARTER OF THE NEGROES   TACIT
ORNETTE AND CONSTERNATION
CLAIM ATTENTION FROM THE PAPERS
THAT HAVE NO NEWS THAT DAY OF MOSCOW.

IN THE POT BEHIND THE

PAPER DOORS WHAT'S COOKING?
WHAT'S SMELLING, LEONTYNE?
LIEDER, LOVELY LIEDER
AND A LEAF OF COLLARD GREEN,
LOVELY LIEDER LEONTYNE.

IN THE SHADOW OF THE NEGROES
   NKRUMAH
IN THE SHADOW OF THE NEGROES
   NASSER NASSER
IN THE SHADOW OF THE NEGROES
   ZIK AZIKIWE
CUBA CASTRO GUINEA TOURÉ
FOR NEED OR PROPAGANDA
   KENYATTA
AND THE TOM DOGS OF THE CABIN
THE COCOA AND THE CANE BRAKE
THE CHAIN GANG AND THE SLAVE BLOCK
TARRED AND FEATHERED NATIONS
SEAGRAM'S AND FOUR ROSES
$5.00 BAGS A DECK OR DAGGA.
FILIBUSTER VERSUS VETO
LIKE A SNAPPING TURTLE—
WON'T LET GO UNTIL IT THUNDERS
WON'T LET GO UNTIL IT THUNDERS
TEARS THE BODY FROM THE SHADOW
WON'T LET GO UNTIL IT THUNDERS
IN THE QUARTER OF THE NEGROES.

AND THEY ASKED ME RIGHT AT CHRISTMAS
IF MY BLACKNESS, WOULD IT RUB OFF?
I SAID, ASK YOUR MAMA.

DREAMS AND NIGHTMARES . . .
NIGHTMARES . . . DREAMS! OH!

Delicate
lieder
on piano
continues
between verses
to merge
softly
into the
melody of the
"Hesitation
Blues" asking
its haunting
question,
"How long
must I
wait?
Can I
get it
now—or
must I
hesitate?"
Suddenly
the drums
roll like
thunder
as the
music ends
sonorously.
TACIT

Figure impishly
into "Dixie"
ending in high
shrill flute call.

DREAMING THAT THE NEGROES   TACIT
OF THE SOUTH HAVE TAKEN OVER—
VOTED ALL THE DIXIECRATS
RIGHT OUT OF POWER—
COMES THE *COLORED HOUR:*
MARTIN LUTHER KING IS GOVERNOR OF GEORGIA,
DR. RUFUS CLEMENT HIS CHIEF ADVISOR,
ZELMA WATSON GEORGE THE HIGH GRAND WORTHY.
IN WHITE PILLARED MANSIONS
SITTING ON THEIR WIDE VERANDAS,
WEALTHY NEGROES HAVE WHITE SERVANTS,
WHITE SHARECROPPERS WORK THE BLACK PLANTATIONS,
AND COLORED CHILDREN HAVE WHITE MAMMIES:

  MAMMY FAUBUS
  MAMMY EASTLAND
  MAMMY PATTERSON.
DEAR, *DEAR* DARLING OLD WHITE MAMMIES—
SOMETIMES EVEN BURIED WITH OUR FAMILY!
  DEAR OLD
  MAMMY FAUBUS!
CULTURE, THEY SAY, *IS A TWO-WAY STREET:*
HAND ME MY MINT JULEP, MAMMY.
  MAKE HASTE!

*"When the Saints
Go Marching In"
joyously for two
full choruses
with maracas. . . .*

2

Ride, Red, Ride

I WANT TO SEE MY MOTHER MOTHER

WHEN THE ROLL IS CALLED UP YONDER

IN THE QUARTER OF THE NEGROES:

   TELL ME HOW LONG—

   MUST I WAIT?

   CAN I GET IT NOW?

   ÇA IRA! ÇA IRA!

   OR MUST I HESITATE?

   IRA! BOY, IRA!

IN THE QUARTER OF THE NEGROES

TU ABUELA, ¿DÓNDE ESTÁ?

LOST IN CASTRO'S BEARD?

TU ABUELA, ¿DÓNDE ESTÁ?

BLOWN SKY HIGH BY MONT PELÉE?

¿DÓNDE ESTÁ? ¿DÓNDE ESTÁ?

WAS SHE FLEEING WITH LUMUMBA?

(GRANDPA'S GRANDMA'S GRANNY

ALWAYS TOOK THE OTHER SIDE.)

A LITTLE RUM WITH SUGAR.

AY, MORENA, ¿DÓNDE ESTÁ?

GRENADINE GRANADA OR

DE SANGRE ES LA GOTA?

SANTA CLAUS, FORGIVE ME,

BUT YOUR GIFT BOOKS ARE SUBVERSIVE.

YOUR DOLLS ARE INTERRACIAL.

YOU'LL BE CALLED BY EASTLAND.

WHEN THEY ASK YOU IF YOU KNEW ME,

Maracas
continue
rhythms
of
"When
the
Saints
Go
Marching
In"
until
the
piano
gently
supplies
a softly
lyrical
calypso
joined now
by the
flute
that ends
in a high
discordant
cry.
TACIT

DON'T TAKE THE FIFTH AMENDMENT.

IN THE QUARTER OF THE NEGROES
RIDING IN A JAGUAR, SANTA CLAUS,
SEEMS LIKE ONCE I MET YOU
WITH ADAM POWELL FOR CHAUFFEUR
AND YOUR HAIR WAS BLOWING BACK
IN THE WIND.

> *Loud and*
> *lively*
> *up-tempo*
> *Dixieland*
> *jazz for*
> *full chorus*
> *to end.*

Shades of Pigmeat

3

IN THE QUARTER OF THE NEGROES   *TACIT*

BELGIUM SHADOWS LEOPOLD

PREMIER DOWNING AGING

GENERAL BOURSE BELEAGUERED

EASTLAND AND MALAN DECEASED

DEAD OR LIVE THEIR GHOSTS CAST SHADOWS

IN THE QUARTER OF THE NEGROES   *Humming:*

WHERE NEGROES SING SO WELL   *"All God's*

NEGROES SING SO WELL   *Chillun*

SING SO WELL   *Got*

SO WELL   *Shoes"*

WELL?

WHERE IS LOTTE LENYA   *TACIT*

AND WHO IS MACK THE KNIFE

AND WAS PORGY EVER MARRIED

BEFORE TAKING BESS TO WIFE

AND WHY WOULD MAI (*NOT MAY*)

BECOME JEWISH

THE HARD

WAY?   *"Eli Eli"*

     merging

IN THE QUARTER OF THE NEGROES   *into a*

ANSWER QUESTIONS ANSWER   *wailing*

AND ANSWERS WITH A QUESTION   *Afro-*

AND THE TALMUD IS CORRECTED   *Arabic*

BY A STUDENT IN A FEZ   *theme*

WHO IS TO JESUIT   *with*

AS NORTH POLE IS TO SOUTH   *flutes*

OR ZIK TO ALABAMA   *and*

OR BIG MAYBELL TO   *steady*

THE MET.

HIP BOOTS
DEEP IN THE BLUES
(AND I NEVER HAD A HIP BOOT ON)
   HAIR
BLOWING BACK IN THE WIND
(AND I NEVER HAD THAT MUCH HAIR)
DIAMONDS IN PAWN
(AND I NEVER HAD A DIAMOND
IN MY NATURAL LIFE)
   ME
IN THE WHITE HOUSE
(AND AIN'T NEVER HAD A BLACK HOUSE)
   DO, JESUS!
   LORD!
   AMEN!

drum beat
changing
into
blues
with
each
instrument
gradually
dropping
out one
by one
leaving
only the
flute at
the end
playing a
whimsical
little
blues of
its own. . . .

4

Ode to Dinah

IN THE QUARTER OF THE NEGROES	TACIT
WHERE TO SNOW NOW ACCLIMATED	
SHADOWS SHOW UP SHARPER,	
THE ONE COIN IN THE METER	
KEEPS THE GAS ON WHILE THE TV	
FAILS TO GET PEARL BAILEY.	
SINCE IT'S SNOWING ON THE TV	
THIS LAST QUARTER OF CENTENNIAL	
100-YEARS EMANCIPATION	
MECHANICS NEED REPAIRING	
FOR NIAGARA FALLS IS FROZEN	
AS IS CUSTOM BELOW ZERO.	
MAMA'S FRUITCAKE SENT FROM GEORGIA	*Traditional*
CRUMBLES AS IT'S NIBBLED	*blues*
TO A DISC BY DINAH	*in gospel*
IN THE RUM THAT WAFTS MARACAS	*tempo*
FROM ANOTHER DISTANT QUARTER	*à la Ray*
TO THIS QUARTER OF THE NEGROES	*Charles*
WHERE THE SONG'S MAHALIA'S DAUGHTER	*to fade*
STEP-FATHERED BY BLIND LEMON	*out*
STEP-FATHERED BY	*slowly. . . .*
BLIND LEMON. . . .	
WHEN NIAGARA FALLS IS FROZEN	TACIT
THERE'S A BAR WITH WINDOWS FROSTED	
FROM THE COLD THAT MAKES NIAGARA	
GHOSTLY MONUMENT OF WINTER	
TO A BAND THAT ONCE PASSED OVER	*Verse of*
WITH A WOMAN WITH TWO PISTOLS	*"Battle*
ON A TRAIN THAT LOST NO PASSENGERS	*Hymn*

97

ON THE LINE WHOSE ROUTE WAS FREEDOM   *of the Republic"*
THROUGH THE JUNGLE OF WHITE DANGER   *through*
TO THE HAVEN OF WHITE QUAKERS   *refrain*
WHOSE HAYMOW WAS A MANGER MANGER   *repeated*
WHERE THE CHRIST CHILD ONCE HAD LAIN.   *ever*
SO THE WHITENESS AND THE WATER   *softer*
MELT TO WATER ONCE AGAIN   *to*
AND THE ROAR OF NIAGARA   *fade*
DROWNS THE RUMBLE OF THAT TRAIN   *out*
DISTANT ALMOST NOW AS DISTANT   *slowly*
AS FORGOTTEN PAIN IN THE QUARTER   *here.*
QUARTER OF THE NEGROES   TACIT
WITH A BAR WITH FROSTED WINDOWS
NO CONDUCTOR AND NO TRAIN.   *Drums*
  BONGO-BONGO! CONGO!   *up strong*
  BUFFALO AND BONGO!   *for*
  NIAGARA OF THE INDIANS!   *interlude*
  NIAGARA OF THE CONGO!   *and out.*

BUFFALO TO HARLEM'S OVERNIGHT: TACIT
IN THE QUARTER OF THE NEGROES
WHERE WHITE SHADOWS PASS,
DARK SHADOWS BECOME DARKER BY A SHADE
SUCKED IN BY FAT JUKEBOXES
WHERE DINAH'S SONGS ARE MADE
FROM SLABS OF SILVER SHADOWS.   *"Hesitation*
AS EACH QUARTER CLINKS   *Blues"*
INTO A MILLION POOLS OF QUARTERS   *softly*
TO BE CARTED OFF BY BRINK'S,   *asking*
THE SHADES OF DINAH'S SINGING   *over*
MAKE A SPANGLE OUT OF QUARTERS RINGING   *and*
TO KEEP FAR-OFF CANARIES   *over*
IN SILVER CAGES SINGING.   *its old*
  TELL ME, PRETTY PAPA,   *question,*
  WHAT TIME IS IT NOW?   *"Tell*

PRETTY PAPA, PRETTY PAPA,

WHAT TIME IS IT NOW?

DON'T CARE WHAT TIME IT IS—

GONNA LOVE YOU ANYHOW

WHILE NIAGARA FALLS IS FROZEN.

SANTA CLAUS, FORGIVE ME,

BUT BABIES BORN IN SHADOWS

IN THE SHADOW OF THE WELFARE

IF BORN PREMATURE

BRING WELFARE CHECKS MUCH SOONER

YET NO PRESENTS DOWN THE CHIMNEY.

IN THE SHADOW OF THE WELFARE

CHOCOLATE BABIES BORN IN SHADOWS

ARE TRIBAL NOW NO LONGER

SAVE IN MEMORIES OF GANGRENOUS ICING

ON A TWENTY-STORY HOUSING PROJECT,

THE CHOCOLATE GANGRENOUS ICING OF

   JUST WAIT.

TRIBAL NOW NO LONGER PAPA MAMA

IN RELATION TO THE CHILD,

ONCE YOUR BROTHER'S KEEPER

NOW NOT EVEN KEEPER TO YOUR CHILD—

SHELTERED NOW NO LONGER,

BORN TO GROW UP WILD—

TRIBAL NOW NO LONGER ONE FOR ALL

AND ALL FOR ONE NO LONGER

EXCEPT IN MEMORIES OF HATE

UMBILICAL IN SULPHUROUS CHOCOLATE:

   GOT TO WAIT—

THIS LAST QUARTER OF CENTENNIAL:

   GOT TO WAIT.

I WANT TO GO TO THE SHOW, MAMA,

---

me

how

long?"

until

music

dies. . . .

TACIT

Drums

alone

softly

merging

into

the

ever-

questioning

"Hesitation

Blues"

beginning

slowly

but

gradually

building to

NO SHOW FARE, BABY—   *up-tempo*
NOT THESE DAYS.   *as the*

                              metronome

ON THE BIG SCREEN OF THE WELFARE CHECK   *of*
A LYNCHED TOMORROW SWAYS. . . .   *fate*
WITH ALL DELIBERATE SPEED A   *begins*
LYNCHED TOMORROW SWAYS.   *to*

                                    tick

LIVING 20 YEARS IN 10   *faster*
BETTER HURRY, BETTER HURRY   *and*
BEFORE THE PRESENT BECOMES WHEN   *faster*
   AND YOU'RE 50   *then*
   WHEN YOU'RE 40   *slowly*
   40 WHEN YOU'RE 30 *retarding*
   30 WHEN YOU'RE 20 *as the*
   20 WHEN YOU'RE 10 *music*
IN THE QUARTER OF THE NEGROES   *dies.*
WHERE THE PENDULUM IS SWINGING
TO THE SHADOW OF THE BLUES,
EVEN WHEN YOU'RE WINNING
THERE'S NO WAY NOT TO LOSE.

WHERE THE SHADOWS MERGE WITH SHADOWS   TACIT
THE DOOR MARKED *LADIES* OPENS INWARD
AND CAN KNOCK THE HADES
OUT OF ONE IN EXIT
IF PUSHED BY HURRIED ENTRANCE.
IN THE SHADOW OF THE QUARTER
WHERE THE PEOPLE ALL ARE DARKER
NOBODY NEEDS A MARKER.
AMEN IS NOT AN ENDING
BUT JUST A PUNCTUATION.
WHITE FOLKS' RECESSION
IS COLORED FOLKS' DEPRESSION.

THEY ASKED ME RIGHT AT CHRISTMAS,
WOULD I MARRY POCAHONTAS?
MEANWHILE DINAH EATING CHICKEN
NEVER MISSED A BITE
WHEN THE MAN SHOT AT THE WOMAN
AND BY MISTAKE SHOT OUT THE LIGHT.

Rim shot.
Dixieland
up-tempo
for full chorus
to ending.

5

Blues in Stereo

YOUR NUMBER'S COMING OUT!   TACIT
BOUQUETS I'LL SEND YOU
AND DREAMS I'LL SEND YOU
AND HORSES SHOD WITH GOLD
ON WHICH TO RIDE IF MOTORCARS
WOULD BE TOO TAME—
TRIUMPHAL ENTRY SEND YOU—
SHOUTS FROM THE EARTH ITSELF
BARE FEET TO BEAT THE GREAT DRUMBEAT
OF GLORY TO YOUR NAME AND MINE
ONE AND THE SAME:
YOU BAREFOOT, TOO,
IN THE QUARTER OF THE NEGROES
WHERE AN ANCIENT RIVER FLOWS
PAST HUTS THAT HOUSE A MILLION BLACKS
AND THE WHITE GOD NEVER GOES
FOR THE MOON WOULD WHITE HIS WHITENESS
BEYOND ITS MASK OF WHITENESS
AND THE NIGHT MIGHT BE ASTONISHED
AND SO LOSE ITS REPOSE.

IN A TOWN NAMED AFTER STANLEY
NIGHT EACH NIGHT COMES NIGHTLY   *African*
AND THE MUSIC OF OLD MUSIC'S   *drum-*
BORROWED FOR THE HORNS   *beats*
THAT DON'T KNOW HOW TO PLAY   *over*
ON LPs THAT WONDER   *blues*
HOW THEY EVER GOT THAT WAY.   *that*
                                        gradually
WHAT TIME IS IT, MAMA?   *mount*

102

WHAT TIME IS IT NOW?   *in*
MAKES NO DIFFERENCE TO ME—   *intensity*
BUT I'M ASKING ANYHOW.   *to*
WHAT TIME IS IT, MAMA?   *end*
WHAT TIME NOW?   *in*
                                   climax.

DOWN THE LONG HARD ROW THAT I BEEN HOEING   TACIT
I THOUGHT I HEARD THE HORN OF PLENTY BLOWING.
BUT I GOT TO GET A NEW ANTENNA, LORD—
MY TV KEEPS ON SNOWING.

Horn of Plenty

```
SINGERS                                          TACIT
SINGERS LIKE O—
SINGERS LIKE ODETTA—AND THAT STATUE
ON BEDLOE'S ISLAND MANAGED BY SOL HUROK
DANCERS BOJANGLES LATE LAMENTED  $ $ $ $ $
KATHERINE DUNHAM AL AND LEON  $ $ $ $ $ $
ARTHUR CARMEN ALVIN MARY  $ $ $ $ $ $ $ $
JAZZERS DUKE AND DIZZY ERIC DOLPHY  $ $ $ $
MILES AND ELLA AND MISS NINA  $ $ $ $ $ $ $
STRAYHORN HID BACKSTAGE WITH LUTHER  $ $
DO YOU READ MUSIC? AND LOUIS SAYING  $ $ $
NOT ENOUGH TO HURT MY PLAYING  $ $ $ $ $ $
GOSPEL SINGERS WHO PANT TO PACK  $ $ $ $ $
GOLDEN CROSSES TO A CADILLAC  $ $ $ $ $ $
BONDS AND STILL AND MARGARET STILL  $ $ $
GLOBAL TROTTERS BASEBALL BATTERS  $ $ $ $
JACKIE WILLIE CAMPANELLA  $ $ $ $ $ $ $ $ $
FOOTBALL PLAYERS LEATHER PUNCHERS  $ $ $
UNFORGOTTEN JOES AND SUGAR RAYS  $ $ $ $ $
WHO BREAK AWAY LIKE COMETS  $ $ $ $ $ $ $
FROM LESSER STARS IN ORBIT  $ $ $ $ $ $ $ $ $
TO MOVE OUT TO ST. ALBANS  $ $ $ $ $ $ $ $ $
WHERE THE GRASS IS GREENER  $ $ $ $ $ $ $ $
SCHOOLS ARE BETTER FOR THEIR CHILDREN  $
AND OTHER KIDS LESS MEANER THAN  ¢ ¢ ¢ ¢
IN THE QUARTER OF THE NEGROES  ¢ ¢ ¢ ¢ ¢ ¢ ¢
WHERE WINTER'S NAME IS HAWKINS  ¢ ¢ ¢ ¢ ¢ ¢
AND NIAGARA FALLS IS FROZEN  ¢ ¢ ¢ ¢ ¢ ¢ ¢ ¢ ¢
IF SHOW FARE'S MORE THAN 30¢  ¢ ¢ ¢ ¢ ¢ ¢ ¢ ¢
```

*"Hesitation
Blues"* 8 bars.

I MOVED OUT TO LONG ISLAND   TACIT
EVEN FARTHER THAN ST. ALBANS
(WHICH LATELY IS STONE NOWHERE)
I MOVED OUT EVEN FARTHER FURTHER FARTHER
ON THE SOUND WAY OFF THE TURNPIKE—
AND I'M THE ONLY COLORED.

GOT THERE! YES, I MADE IT!
NAME IN THE PAPERS EVERY DAY!
FAMOUS—THE HARD WAY—
FROM NOBODY AND NOTHING TO WHERE I AM.
THEY KNOW ME, TOO, DOWNTOWN,
ALL ACROSS THE COUNTRY, EUROPE—
ME WHO USED TO BE NOBODY,
NOTHING BUT ANOTHER SHADOW
IN THE QUARTER OF THE NEGROES,
NOW A NAME! MY NAME—A NAME!

YET THEY ASKED ME OUT ON MY PATIO
WHERE DID I GET MY MONEY!
I SAID, FROM YOUR MAMA!   *Figurine.*
THEY WONDERED WAS I SENSITIVE
AND HAD A CHIP ON SHOULDER?
DID I KNOW CHARLIE MINGUS?
AND WHY DID RICHARD WRIGHT
LIVE ALL THAT WHILE IN PARIS
INSTEAD OF COMING HOME TO DECENT DIE
IN HARLEM OR THE SOUTH SIDE OF CHICAGO
OR THE WOMB OF MISSISSIPPI?
AND ONE SHOULD LOVE ONE'S COUNTRY
FOR ONE'S COUNTRY IS YOUR MAMA.

LIVING IN ST. ALBANS
SHADOW OF THE NEGROES
WESTPORT AND NEW CANAAN

IN THE SHADOW OF THE NEGROES—
HIGHLY INTEGRATED
MEANS TOO MANY NEGROES
EVEN FOR THE NEGROES—
ESPECIALLY FOR THE FIRST ONES
WHO MOVE IN UNOBTRUSIVE   *Gently*
BOOK-OF-THE-MONTH IN CASES   *yearning*
SEEKING SUBURB WITH NO JUKEBOX   *lieder*
POOL HALL OR BAR ON CORNER   *on*
SEEKING LAWNS AND SHADE TREES   *piano,*
SEEKING PEACE AND QUIET   *delicately*
AUTUMN LEAVES IN AUTUMN   *sedate,*
HOLLAND BULBS IN SPRING   *quietly*
DECENT GARBAGE SERVICE   *fading*
BIRDS THAT REALLY SING   *on the*
$40,000 HOUSES—   *word*
PAYMENTS NOT BELATED—   *belated.* . . .
THE ONLY NEGROES IN THE BLOCK   TACIT
INTEGRATED.

HORN OF PLENTY   *Again*
IN ESCROW TO JOE GLASSER.   *the old*
THE SERMON ON THE MOUNT   *"Hesitation*
IN BILLINGTON'S CHURCH OF RUBBER. *Blues"*
LOVE THY NEIGHBOR AS THYSELF   *against the*
IN GEORGE SOKOLSKY'S COLUMN.   *trills*
BIRDS THAT REALLY SING.   *of birds,*
EVERY DAY'S TOMORROW   *but the*
AND ELECTION TIME   *melody*
IS ALWAYS FOUR YEARS   *ends in*
FROM THE OTHER   *a thin*
AND MY LAWN MOWER   *high*
NEW AND SHINY   *flute call.*
FROM THE BIG GLASS SHOPPING CENTER
CUTS MY HAIR ON CREDIT.

THEY RUNG MY BELL TO ASK ME
COULD I RECOMMEND A MAID.
I SAID, YES, YOUR MAMA.

TACIT

Figurine.

7

Gospel Cha-Cha

IN THE QUARTER OF THE NEGROES	
WHERE THE PALMS AND COCONUTS	
CHA-CHA LIKE CASTANETS	*Maracas . . .*
IN THE WIND'S FRENETIC FISTS	*in*
WHERE THE SAND SEEDS AND THE	*cha-cha*
SEA GOURDS MAKE MARACAS OUT OF ME,	*tempo,*
ERZULIE PLAYS A TUNE	*then*
ON THE BONGO OF THE MOON.	*bongo drums*
THE PAPA DRUM OF SUN	*joined*
AND THE MOTHER DRUM OF EARTH	*by*
KNOW TOURISTS ONLY FOR	*the*
THE MONEY THAT THEY'RE WORTH	*piano,*
IN THE QUARTER OF THE NEGROES	*guitar*
MAMA MAMACITA PAPA PAPIAMENTO	*and*
DAMBALLA WEDO OGOUN AND THE HORSE	*claves,*
THAT LUGGED THE FIRST WHITE	*eerie*
FIRST WHITE TOURIST UP THE MOUNTAIN	*and*
TO THE CITADELLE OF SHADOWS SHADOWS	*strange*
WHERE THE SHADOWS OF THE NEGROES	*like*
ARE THE GHOSTS OF FORMER GLORY	*bones*
TOUSSAINT WITH A THREAD	*rattling*
THREAD STILL PULLS HIS	*in a*
PROW OF STONE STONE.	*sort*
I BOIL A FISH AND SALT IT	*of off-*
(AND MY PLANTAINS)	*beat mambo*
WITH HIS GLORY.	*up strong*
	between verses
¡AY, BAHIA!	*then*
¡AY, BAHIA!	*down*

SUNSETS STAINED WITH BLOOD   *under*
CLEAR GREEN CRYSTAL WATER   *voice*
AND THE CRY THAT TURNED TO MUSIC   *to*
WHERE THE SEA SAND AND THE SEA GOURDS   *gradually*
MAKE CLAVES OF MY SORROWS   *die away*
IN THE WIND'S FRENETIC FISTS.   *in the*
MAMACITA! PAPA LEGBA! SHANGO!   *lonely*
BEDWARD! POCOMANIA! WEDO! OGOUN!   *swish-*
THE BOAT BEYOND THE FORTALEZA   *swish of*
TO THE VILLE OF NAÑIGO.   *the*
A LONG WAY TO BAHIA—   *maracas. . . .*
HOW I GOT THERE I DON'T KNOW.   TACIT
WHAT'S HIS NAME, MY COUSIN,
WHO SEDUCED MARIE LAVEAU?
DAMBALLA WEDO! THE VIRGIN! BEDWARD!
JOHN JASPER! JESUS! DADDY GRACE!   *Gospel*
  I TRIED   *music*
  LORD KNOWS I TRIED   *with a*
  DAMBALLA   *very*
  I PRAYED   *heavy*
  LORD KNOWS I PRAYED   *beat*
  DADDY   *as if*
  I CLIMBED   *marching*
  UP THAT STEEP HILL   *forward*
  THE VIRGIN   *against*
  WITH A CROSS   *great*
  LORD KNOWS I CLIMBED   *odds,*
  BUT WHEN I GOT   *climbing*
  JOHN JASPER JESUS   *a*
  WHEN I GOT TO CALVARY   *high*
  UP THERE ON THAT HILL   *hill—*
  ALREADY THERE WAS THREE—   *to again*
  AND ONE, YES, ONE   *fade into*
  WAS BLACK AS ME.   *the dry*

*swish of
maracas
in cha-cha
time.*

*CHA-CHA . . . CHA-CHA
CHA. . . .*

Is It True?

FROM THE SHADOWS OF THE QUARTER   TACIT
SHOUTS ARE WHISPERS CARRYING
TO THE FARTHEREST CORNERS SOMETIMES
OF THE NOW KNOWN WORLD
UNDECIPHERED AND UNLETTERED
UNCODIFIED UNPARSED
IN TONGUES UNANALYZED UNECHOED
UNTAKEN DOWN ON TAPE—
NOT EVEN FOLKWAYS CAPTURED
BY MOE ASCH OR ALAN LOMAX
NOT YET ON SAFARI.
WHERE GAME TO BAG'S ILLUSIVE
AS A SILVER UNICORN
AND THE GUN TO DO THE KILLING'S
STILL TO BE INVENTED,
TO FERTILIZE THE DESERT
THE FRENCH MAY HAVE THE SECRET.   *Deep*
TURN, OH, TURN, DARK LOVERS   *drum*
ON YOUR BED OF WHISPERED ECHOES: *vibrato*
   ¡AY, DIOS!   *into a*
     ¡AY, DIOS!   *single high*
       ¡AY, DIOS!   *flute*
                     note. . . .

TWENTY HOURS   TACIT
FOR THE MILL WHEEL TO BE MILL WHEEL
WAITED TWENTY DAYS
FOR THE BISQUIT TO BE BREAD
WAITED TWENTY YEARS
FOR THE SADNESS TO BE SORROW,

WAITED TWENTY MORE
TO CATCH UP WITH TOMORROW
AND I CANNOT WRITE COMMERCIALS—
TO MY CHAGRIN—NOT EVEN SINGING—
AND THE WHISPERS ARE UNECHOED
ON THE TAPES—NOT EVEN FOLKWAYS.

YES, SUBURBIA
WILL EVENTUALLY BE
ONLY IN THE SEA. . . .
MEANWHILE
OF COURSE
OF COURSE
OF COURSE
ON A MUDDY TRACK
IN THE QUARTER OF THE NEGROES
NEGROES
NEGROES
SOME HORSE MIGHT
SLIP AND BREAK
ITS BACK:
BUT SCRIPT-WRITERS WHO KNOW BETTER
WOULD HARDLY WRITE IT IN THE SCRIPT—
OR SPORTS-WRITERS IN THEIR STORY.
YET THE HORSE WHOSE BACK IS BROKEN
GETS SHOT RIGHT INTO GLORY.

THEY ASKED ME AT THE PTA
IS IT TRUE THAT NEGROES—?
I SAID, ASK YOUR MAMA.

High
flute
call.

Ask Your Mama

9

FROM THE SHADOWS OF THE QUARTER
SHOUTS ARE WHISPERS CARRYING
TO THE FARTHEREST CORNERS
OF THE NOW KNOWN WORLD:
5th AND MOUND IN CINCI, 63rd IN CHI,
23rd AND CENTRAL, 18th STREET AND VINE.
I'VE WRITTEN, CALLED REPEATEDLY,
EVEN RUNG THIS BELL ON SUNDAY, YET
YOUR THIRD-FLOOR TENANT'S NEVER HOME.
DID YOU TELL HER THAT OUR CREDIT OFFICE
HAS NO RECOURSE NOW BUT TO THE LAW?
YES, SIR, I TOLD HER.
WHAT DID SHE SAY?
SAID, TELL YOUR MA.   *Figurine.*

17 SORROWS
AND THE NUMBER
6–0–2.
HIGH BALLS, LOW BALLS:
THE 8-BALL
IS YOU.
7–11!
COME 7!
PORGY AND BESS
AT THE PICTURE SHOW.
I NEVER SEEN IT.
BUT I WILL,
YOU KNOW,
IF I HAVE
THE MONEY

TO GO.	*Delicate*
	post-bop
FILLMORE OUT IN FRISCO, 7th ACROSS THE BAY,	*suggests*
18th AND VINE IN K. C., 63rd IN CHI,	*pleasant*
ON THE CORNER PICKING SPLINTERS	*evenings and*
OUT OF THE MIDNIGHT SKY	*flirtatious*
IN THE QUARTER OF THE NEGROES	*youth*
AS LEOLA PASSES BY	*as it*
THE MEN CAN ONLY MURMUR	*gradually*
MY! . . . *MY! MY!*	*weaves*
	into its
LUMUMBA LOUIS ARMSTRONG	*pattern*
PATRICE AND PATTI PAGE	*a*
HAMBURGERS PEPSI-COLA	*musical*
KING COLE JUKEBOX PAYOLA	*echo of*
IN THE QUARTER OF THE NEGROES	*Paris*
GOD WILLING DROP A SHILLING	*which*
FORT DE FRANCE, PLACE PIGALLE	*continues*
VINGT FRANCS NICKEL DIME	*until*
BAHIA LAGOS DAKAR LENOX	*very*
KINGSTON TOO GOD WILLING	*softly*
A QUARTER OR A SHILLING. PARIS—	*the*
AT THE DOME VINGT FRANCS WILL DO	*silver*
ROTONDE SELECT DUPONT FLORE	*call*
TALL BLACK STUDENT	*of a*
IN HORN-RIM GLASSES,	*hunting*
WHO AT THE SORBONNE HAS SIX CLASSES,	*horn*
IN THE SHADOW OF THE CLUNY	*is*
CONJURES UNICORN,	*heard*
SPEAKS ENGLISH FRENCH SWAHILI	*far away.*
HAS ALMOST FORGOTTEN MEALIE.	*African*
BUT WHY RIDE ON MULE OR DONKEY	*drums*
WHEN THERE'S A UNICORN?	*begin*
	a softly
NIGHT IN A SÉKOU TOURÉ CAP	*mounting*

DRESSED LIKE A TEDDY BOY   *rumble*
BLOTS COLORS OFF THE MAP.   *soon*
PERHAPS IF IT BE GOD'S WILL   *to fade*
AZIKIWE'S SON, AMEKA,   *into a*
SHAKES HANDS WITH EMMETT TILL.   *steady*
BRICKBATS BURST LIKE BUBBLES   *beat*
STONES BURST LIKE BALLOONS   *like*
BUT HEARTS KEEP DOGGED BEATING   *the*
   SELDOM BURSTING   *heart.*
   UNLIKE BUBBLES
   UNLIKE BRICKBATS   TACIT
   FAR FROM STONE.
IN THE QUARTER OF THE NEGROES
WHERE NO SHADOW WALKS ALONE
LITTLE MULES AND DONKEYS SHARE
THEIR GRASS WITH UNICORNS.   *Repeat high*
                                            flute call
                                            to segue into
                                            up-tempo blues
                                            that continue
                                            behind the
                                            next sequence. . . .

10

Bird in Orbit

DE—   *Happy*

DELIGHT—   *blues*

DELIGHTED! INTRODUCE ME TO EARTHA   *in*

JOCKO BODDIDLY LIL GREENWOOD   *up-beat*

BELAFONTE FRISCO JOSEPHINE   *tempo*

BRICKTOP INEZ MABEL MERCER   *trip*

AND I'D LIKE TO MEET THE   *merrily*

ONE-TIME SIX-YEAR-OLDS   *along*

FIRST GRADE IN NEW ORLEANS   *until*

IN THE QUARTER OF THE NEGROES   *the music*

WHERE SIT-INS ARE CONDUCTED   *suddenly*

BY THOSE YET UNINDUCTED   *stops in*

AND BALLOTS DROP IN BOXES   *a loud*

WHERE BULLETS ARE THE TELLERS.   *rim shot.*

THEY ASKED ME AT THANKSGIVING   TACIT

DID I VOTE FOR NIXON?

I SAID, VOTED FOR YOUR MAMA.   *Figurine.*

METHUSELAH SIGNS PAPERS W. E. B.   *Cool*

ORIGINAL NIAGARA N.A.A.C.P.   *bop*

ADELE RAMONA MICHAEL SERVE BAKOKO TEA   *very*

IRENE AND HELEN ARE AS THEY USED TO BE   *light*

AND SMITTY HAS NOT CHANGED AT ALL.   *and*

ALIOUNE AIMÉ SEDAR SIPS HIS NEGRITUDE.   *delicate*

THE REVEREND MARTIN LUTHER   *rising*

KING MOUNTS HIS UNICORN   *to an*

OBLIVIOUS TO BLOOD   *ethereal*

AND MOONLIGHT ON ITS HORN   *climax . . .*

WHILE MOLLIE MOON STREWS SEQUINS   *completely*

AS LEDA STREW HER CORN   *far*
AND CHARLIE YARDBIRD PARKER   *out. . . .*
IS IN ORBIT.

   ¡AY, MI NEGRA!   TACIT
   ¡AY, MORENA!

GRANDPA, WHERE DID YOU MEET MY GRANDMA?
AT MOTHER BETHEL'S IN THE MORNING?
I'M ASKING, GRANDPA, ASKING.
WERE YOU MARRIED BY JOHN JASPER
OF THE DO-MOVE COSMIC CONSCIENCE?
GRANDPA, DID YOU HEAR THE
HEAR THE OLD FOLKS SAY HOW
HOW TALL HOW TALL THE CANE GREW
SAY HOW WHITE THE COTTON COTTON
SPEAK OF RICE DOWN IN THE MARSHLAND
SPEAK OF FREDERICK DOUGLASS'S BEARD
AND JOHN BROWN'S WHITE AND LONGER   *"The*
LINCOLN'S LIKE A CLOTHESBRUSH   *Battle*
AND OF HOW SOJOURNER HOW SOJOURNER   *Hymn*
TO PROVE SHE WAS A WOMAN WOMAN   *of*
BARED HER BOSOMS, BARED IN PUBLIC   *the*
TO PROVE SHE WAS A WOMAN?   *Republic"*
WHAT SHE SAID ABOUT HER CHILDREN   *as a*
ALL SOLD DOWN THE RIVER.   *flute*
I LOOK AT THE STARS   *solo*
AND THEY LOOK AT THE STARS,   *soft*
AND THEY WONDER WHERE I BE   *and*
AND I WONDER WHERE THEY BE.   *far*
STARS AT STARS STARS. . . .   *away*
   TOURÉ DOWN IN GUINEA   *fading*
   LUMUMBA IN THE CONGO   *in the*
   JOMO IN KENYATTA. . . . STARS. . . .   *distance. . . .*
GRANDPA, DID YOU FIND HER IN THE TV SILENCE   TACIT

OF A MILLION MARTHA ROUNDTREES?
IN THE QUARTER OF THE NEGROES
DID YOU EVER FIND HER?

THAT GENTLEMAN IN EXPENSIVE SHOES
MADE FROM THE HIDES OF BLACKS
WHO TIPS AMONG THE SHADOWS
SOAKING UP THE MUSIC
ASKED ME RIGHT AT CHRISTMAS
DID I WANT TO EAT WITH WHITE FOLKS?   *Flute cry. . . .*

THOSE SIT-IN KIDS, HE SAID,   TACIT
   MUST BE RED!
KENYATTA RED! CASTRO RED!
   NKRUMAH RED!
RALPH BUNCHE INVESTIGATED!
MARY McLEOD BETHUNE BARRED BY
THE LEGION FROM ENGLEWOOD
NEW JERSEY HIGH SCHOOL!
HOW ABOUT THAT N.A.A.C.P.
AND THE RADICALS IN THAT
THERE SOUTHERN CONFERENCE?
AIN'T YOU GOT NO INFORMATION
ON DR. ROBERT WEAVER?
INVESTIGATE THAT SANTA CLAUS
WHOSE DOLLS ARE INTERRACIAL!
INVESTIGATE THEM NEGRAS WHO
BOUGHT A DOBERMAN PINSCHER.   *Flute*
                                                       call
THAT GENTLEMAN IN EXPENSIVE SHOES   *into*
MADE FROM THE HIDES OF BLACKS   *very*
TIPS AMONG THE SHADOWS   *far-out*
SOAKING UP THE MUSIC. . . .   *boopish*
MUSIC. . . .   *blues. . . .*

Jazztet Muted

IN THE NEGROES OF THE QUARTER	*Bop*
PRESSURE OF THE BLOOD IS SLIGHTLY HIGHER	*blues*
IN THE QUARTER OF THE NEGROES	*into*
WHERE BLACK SHADOWS MOVE LIKE SHADOWS	*very*
CUT FROM SHADOWS CUT FROM SHADE	*modern*
IN THE QUARTER OF THE NEGROES	*jazz*
SUDDENLY CATCHING FIRE	*burning*
FROM THE WING TIP OF A MATCH TIP	*the*
ON THE BREATH OF ORNETTE COLEMAN.	*air*
	eerie
IN NEON TOMBS THE MUSIC	*like*
FROM JUKEBOX JOINTS IS LAID	*a neon*
AND FREE-DELIVERY TV SETS	*swamp-*
ON GRAVESTONES DATES ARE PLAYED.	*fire*
EXTRA-LARGE THE *KINGS* AND *QUEENS*	*cooled*
AT EITHER SIDE ARRAYED	*by*
HAVE DOORS THAT OPEN OUTWARD	*dry*
TO THE QUARTER OF THE NEGROES	*ice*
WHERE THE PRESSURE OF THE BLOOD	*until*
IS SLIGHTLY HIGHER—	*suddenly*
DUE TO SMOLDERING SHADOWS	*there is*
THAT SOMETIMES TURN TO FIRE.	*a single*
	ear-
HELP ME, YARDBIRD!	*piercing*
HELP ME!	*flute*
	call. . . .

Show Fare, Please

TELL ME MAMA, CAN I GET MY SHOW   TACIT
TELL ME FARE FROM YOU?
OR DO YOU THINK THAT PAPA'S
GOT CHANGE IN HIS LONG POCKET?
IN THE QUARTER OF THE NEGROES
WHERE THE MASK IS PLACED BY OTHERS
IBM ELECTRIC BONGO DRUMS ARE COSTLY.
TELL ME, MAMA, TELL ME,   *Rhythmic*
STRIP TICKETS STILL ILLUSION?   *bop,*
GOT TO ASK YOU—GOT TO ASK!   *ever*
TELL ME, TELL ME, MAMA,   *more*
ALL THAT MUSIC, ALL THAT DANCING   *ironic,*
CONCENTRATED TO THE ESSENCE   *laughs*
OF THE SHADOW OF A DOLLAR   *itself*
PAID AT THE BOX OFFICE   *softly*
WHERE THE LIGHTER IS THE DARKER   *into a*
IN THE QUARTER OF THE NEGROES   *lonely*
AND THE TELL ME OF THE MAMA   *flute*
IS THE ANSWER TO THE CHILD.   *call. . . .*

DID YOU EVER SEE TEN NEGROES
WEAVING METAL FROM TWO QUARTERS
INTO CLOTH OF DOLLARS
FOR A SUIT OF GOOD-TIME WEARING?
WEAVING OUT OF LONG-TERM CREDIT
INTEREST BEYOND CARING?

THE HEADS ON THESE TWO QUARTERS
ARE *THIS* OR *THAT*
OR *LESS* OR *MOST*—

SINCE BUT TWO EXIST
BEYOND THE HOLY GHOST.
OF THESE THREE,
IS ONE
ME?

THE TV'S STILL NOT WORKING.
SHOW FARE, MAMA, PLEASE.
SHOW FARE, MAMA. . . .
SHOW FARE!

*"The Hesitation
Blues" very loud,
lively and
raucously. Two
big swinging
choruses—
building full
blast to a
bursting climax.*

Liner Notes
For the Poetically Unhep

Cultural Exchange

In Negro sections of the South where doors have no resistance to violence, danger always whispers harshly. Klansmen cavort, and havoc may come at any time. Negroes often live either by the river or the railroad, and for most there is not much chance of going anywhere else. Yet *always* one of them has been away and has come home. The door has opened to admit something strange and foreign, yet tied by destiny to a regional past nourished by a way of life in common—in this case collard greens.

A State Department visitor from Africa comes, wishing to meet Negroes. He is baffled by the "two sides to every question" way of looking at things in the South. Although he finds that in the American social supermarket blacks for sale range from intellectuals to entertainers, to the African all cellophane signs point to ideas of change—in an IBM land that pays more attention to Moscow than to Mississippi.

What—wonders the African—is really happening in the shadow of world events, past and present—and of world problems, old and new—to an America that seems to understand so little about its black citizens? Even so little about itself. Even so little.

Ride, Red, Ride

In the restless Caribbean there are the same shadows as in Mississippi, where, according to *Time,* Leontyne comes in the back door. Yet some persons in high places in Washington consider it subversive for ordinary people to be concerned with problems such as back doors anywhere— even suspecting those citizens of color who legitimately use the ballot in the North to elect representatives to front doors. But in spite of all, some Negroes occasionally do manage—for a moment—to get a brief ride in somebody's American chariot.

Shades of Pigmeat

Oppression by any other name is just about the same, casts a long shadow, adds a dash of bitters to each song, makes of almost every answer a question, and of men of every race or religion questioners.

Ode to Dinah

Hard times endure from slavery to freedom—to Harlem where most of the money spent goes downtown. Only a little comes back in the form of relief checks, which leaves next to nothing for show fare for children who must live in a hurry in order to live at all. Yet in a milieu where so many untoward things happen, one cannot afford to take to heart too deeply the hazards. Remember Harriet Tubman? One of the runaway slaves in her band was so frightened crossing from Buffalo into Canada that on the very last lap of his journey he hid under the seat of the train and refused to glance out the window. Harriet said: "You old fool! Even on your way to freedom, you might at least look at Niagara Falls."

Blues in Stereo

Sometimes you are lucky, or at least you can dream lucky—even if you wake up cold in hand. But maybe with a new antenna you will get a clearer picture.

Horn of Plenty

Certainly there are some who make money—and others whom folks *think* make money. It takes money to buy gas to commute to the suburbs and keep one's lawns sheared like one's white neighbors who wonder how on earth a Negro got a lawn mower in the face of so many ways of keeping him from getting a lawn.

Gospel Cha-Cha

Those who have no lawns to mow seek gods who come in various spiritual and physical guises and to whom one prays in various rhythms in various lands in various tongues.

Is It True?

It seems as if everything is annotated one way or another, but the subtler nuances remain to be captured. However, the atom bomb may solve all this—since it would end the end results of love's own annotation. Meanwhile, although the going is rough, triumph over difficulties at least brings subjective glory. Everybody thinks that Negroes have the *most* fun, but, of course, secretly hopes they do not—although curious to find out if they do.

Ask Your Mama

In spite of a shortage of funds for the movies and the frequent rude intrusions of those concerned with hoarding hard metals, collective coins for music-making and grass for dreams to graze on still keep men, mules, donkeys, and black students alive.

Bird in Orbit

Those who contribute most to the joy of living and the stretching of the social elastic are not stymied by foolish questions, but keep right on drawing from the well of the past buckets of water in which to catch stars. In their pockets are layovers for meddlers—although somewhere grandma lost her apron.

Jazztet Muted

Because grandma lost her apron with all the answers in her pocket (perhaps consumed by fire) certain grand- and great-grandsons play music burning like dry ice against the ear. Forcing cries of succor from its own unheard completion—not resolved by Charlie Parker—can we look to monk or Monk? Or let it rest with Eric Dolphy?

Show Fare, Please

If the answers were on tickets in long strips like those that come from slots inside the cashier's booth at the movies, and if I had the money for a ticket—like the man who owns *all* tickets, *all* booths, and *all* movies and who pays the ticket seller who in turn charges me—would I, with answer in my hand, become one of the three—the man, the ticket seller, me? Show fare, mama, please. . . .

The Panther and the Lash

Poems of Our Times

(1967)

Certain poems in this collection were previously published in the following books by Langston Hughes:

Ask Your Mama (1961): "Cultural Exchange"

Fields of Wonder (1947): "Words Like Freedom," "Oppression," "Dream Dust"

The Langston Hughes Reader (1958): "Elderly Leaders" under the title "Elderly Politicians"

Montage of a Dream Deferred (1951): "Corner Meeting," "Motto," "Children's Rhymes"

One-Way Ticket (1949): "Harlem" under the title "Puzzled," "Who But the Lord?," "Third Degree," "October 16: The Raid," "Still Here," "Florida Road Workers," "Freedom" under the title "Democracy," "Warning" under the title "Roland Hayes Beaten," "Daybreak in Alabama"

Scottsboro Limited (1932): "Christ in Alabama," "Justice"

Selected Poems of Langston Hughes (1959): "Dream Deferred" under the title "Harlem," "American Heartbreak," "Georgia Dusk," "Jim Crow Car" under the title "Lunch in a Jim Crow Car"

Shakespeare in Harlem (1942): "Ku Klux," "Merry-Go-Round"

The author wishes to thank the editors of the following publications which first printed the poems specified:

American Dialog: "Final Call" (1964)
Black Orpheus: "Angola Question Mark" (1959)
Colorado Review: "Where? When? Which?" (Winter 1956–1957)
Crisis: "Question and Answer" (1966)
Free Lance: "Without Benefit of Declaration" (1955)
Harper's Magazine: "Long View: Negro" (1965)
Liberator: "Junior Addict" (1963), "Frederick Douglass" (1966), "Northern Liberal" (1963)
The Nation: "Crowns and Garlands" (1967)
Negro Digest: "Mississippi" (1965), "Dinner Guest: Me" (1965)
Opportunity: "History" (1934)
Phylon: "Little Song on Housing" (1955), "Vari-Colored Song" (1952)
Le Poesie Negro-Americaine (1966): "Bible Belt" under the title "Not for Publication—Defense de Publier"
Voices: "Down Where I Am" (1950)

To Rosa Parks of Montgomery

who started it all when, on being ordered to get up and stand at the back of the bus where there were no seats left, she said simply, "My feet are tired," and did not move, thus setting off in 1955 the boycotts, the sit-ins, the Freedom Rides, the petitions, the marches, the voter registration drives, and *I Shall Not Be Moved.*

Contents

3. The Bible Belt

4. The Face of War

5. African Question Mark

1

Words on Fire

Corner Meeting

Ladder, flag, and amplifier
now are what the soap box
used to be.

The speaker catches fire,
looking at listeners' faces.

His words jump down
to stand
in their
places.

Harlem

Here on the edge of hell
Stands Harlem—
Remembering the old lies,
The old kicks in the back,
The old "Be patient"
They told us before.

Sure, we remember.
Now when the man at the corner store
Says sugar's gone up another two cents,
And bread one,
And there's a new tax on cigarettes—
We remember the job we never had,
Never could get,

And can't have now
Because we're colored.

So we stand here
On the edge of hell
In Harlem
And look out on the world
And wonder
What we're gonna do
In the face of what
We remember.

Prime

Uptown on Lenox Avenue
Where a nickel costs a dime,
In these lush and thieving days
When million-dollar thieves
Glorify their million-dollar ways
In the press and on the radio and TV—
    But won't let me
    Skim even a dime—
I, black, come to my prime
In the section of the niggers
Where a nickel costs a dime.

Crowns and Garlands

Make a garland of Leontynes and Lenas
And hang it about your neck
    Like a lei.
Make a crown of Sammys, Sidneys, Harrys,
Plus Cassius Mohammed Ali Clay.

Put their laurels on your brow
   Today—
Then before you can walk
To the neighborhood corner,
Watch them droop, wilt, fade
   Away.
Though worn in glory on my head,
They do not last a day—
   Not one—
Nor take the place of meat or bread
Or rent that I must pay.
Great names for crowns and garlands!
   Yeah!
I love Ralph Bunche—
But I can't eat him for lunch.

Elderly Leaders

The old, the cautious, the over-wise—
Wisdom reduced to the personal equation:
Life is a system of half-truths and lies,
Opportunistic, convenient evasion.
   Elderly,
   Famous,
   Very well paid,
   They clutch at the egg
   Their master's
   Goose laid:
   $$$$$
   $$$$
   $$$
   $$
   $
   •

The Backlash Blues

Mister Backlash, Mister Backlash,
Just who do you think I am?
Tell me, Mister Backlash,
Who do you think I am?
You raise my taxes, freeze my wages,
Send my son to Vietnam.

You give me second-class houses,
Give me second-class schools,
Second-class houses
And second-class schools.
You must think us colored folks
Are second-class fools.

When I try to find a job
To earn a little cash,
Try to find myself a job
To earn a little cash,
All you got to offer
Is a white backlash.

But the world is big,
The world is big and round,
Great big world, Mister Backlash,
Big and bright and round—
And it's full of folks like me who are
Black, Yellow, Beige, and Brown.

Mister Backlash, Mister Backlash,
What do you think I got to lose?
Tell me, Mister Backlash,
What you think I got to lose?
I'm gonna leave you, Mister Backlash,
Singing your mean old backlash blues.

You're the one,
Yes, you're the one
Will have the blues.

Lenox Avenue Bar

Weaving
between assorted terrors
is the Jew
who owns the place—
one Jew,
fifty Negroes:
embroideries
(heirloomed
from ancient evenings)
tattered
in this neon
place.

Motto

I play it cool
And dig all jive—
That's the reason
I stay alive.

My motto,
As I live and learn
   Is
Dig and be dug
In return.

Junior Addict

The little boy
who sticks a needle in his arm
and seeks an out in other worldly dreams,
who seeks an out in eyes that droop
and ears that close to Harlem screams,
cannot know, of course,
(and has no way to understand)
a sunrise that he cannot see
beginning in some other land—
but destined sure to flood—and soon—
the very room in which he leaves
his needle and his spoon,
the very room in which today the air
is heavy with the drug
of his despair.

   (Yet little can
   tomorrow's sunshine give
   to one who will not live.)

Quick, sunrise, come—
Before the mushroom bomb
Pollutes his stinking air
With better death
Than is his living here,
With viler drugs
Than bring today's release
In poison from the fallout
Of our peace.

   "It's easier to get dope
   than it is to get a job."

Yes, easier to get dope
than to get a job—
daytime or nighttime job,
teen-age, pre-draft,
pre-lifetime job.

Quick, sunrise, come!
Sunrise out of Africa,
Quick, come!
Sunrise, please come!
Come! Come!

Dream Deferred

What happens to a dream deferred?

   Does it dry up
   like a raisin in the sun?
   Or fester like a sore—
   And then run?
   Does it stink like rotten meat?
   Or crust and sugar over—
   like a syrupy sweet?

   Maybe it just sags
   like a heavy load.

   Or does it explode?

Death in Yorkville

(James Powell, Summer, 1964)

How many bullets does it take
To kill a fifteen-year-old kid?
How many bullets does it take
To kill me?

How many centuries does it take
To bind my mind—chain my feet—
Rope my neck—lynch me—
Unfree?

From the slave chain to the lynch rope
To the bullets of Yorkville,
Jamestown, 1619 to 1963:
Emancipation Centennial—
100 years NOT free.

Civil War Centennial: 1965.
How many Centennials does it take
To kill me,
Still alive?

When the long hot summers come
Death ain't
No jive.

Who But the Lord?

I looked and I saw
That man they call the Law.
He was coming
Down the street at me!
I had visions in my head

Of being laid out cold and dead,
Or else murdered
By the third degree.

I said, *O, Lord, if you can,*
Save me from that man!
Don't let him make a pulp out of me!
But the Lord he was not quick.
The Law raised up his stick
And beat the living hell
Out of me!

Now I do not understand
Why God don't protect a man
From police brutality.
Being poor and black,
I've no weapon to strike back
So who but the Lord
Can protect me?

   We'll see.

Third Degree

Hit me! Jab me!
Make me say I did it.
Blood on my sport shirt
And my tan suede shoes.

Faces like jack-o'-lanterns
In gray slouch hats.

Slug me! Beat me!
Scream jumps out
Like blowtorch.

Three kicks between the legs
That kill the kids
I'd make tomorrow.

Bars and floor skyrocket
And burst like Roman candles.

When you throw
Cold water on me,
I'll sign the
Paper . . .

Black Panther

Pushed into the corner
Of the hobnailed boot,
Pushed into the corner of the
"I-don't-want-to-die" cry,
Pushed into the corner of
"I don't want to study war no more,"
Changed into "Eye for eye,"
The Panther in his desperate boldness
Wears no disguise,
Motivated by the truest
Of the oldest
Lies.

Final Call

SEND FOR THE PIED PIPER AND LET HIM PIPE THE RATS
   AWAY.
SEND FOR ROBIN HOOD TO CLINCH THE ANTI-POVERTY
   CAMPAIGN.

SEND FOR THE FAIRY QUEEN WITH A WAVE OF THE WAND
TO MAKE US ALL INTO PRINCES AND PRINCESSES.
SEND FOR KING ARTHUR TO BRING THE HOLY GRAIL.
SEND FOR OLD MAN MOSES TO LAY DOWN THE LAW.
SEND FOR JESUS TO PREACH THE SERMON ON THE MOUNT.
SEND FOR DREYFUS TO CRY, *"J'ACCUSE!"*
SEND FOR DEAD BLIND LEMON TO SING THE *B FLAT BLUES.*
SEND FOR ROBESPIERRE TO SCREAM, *"ÇA IRA! ÇA IRA! ÇA
    IRA!"*
SEND (GOD FORBID—HE'S NOT DEAD LONG ENOUGH!)
FOR LUMUMBA TO CRY "FREEDOM NOW!"
SEND FOR LAFAYETTE AND TELL HIM, "HELP! HELP ME!"
SEND FOR DENMARK VESEY CRYING, "FREE!"
FOR CINQUE SAYING, "RUN A NEW FLAG UP THE MAST."
FOR OLD JOHN BROWN WHO KNEW SLAVERY COULDN'T
    LAST.
SEND FOR LENIN! (DON'T YOU DARE!—HE CAN'T COME
    HERE!)
SEND FOR TROTSKY! (WHAT? DON'T CONFUSE THE ISSUE,
    PLEASE!)
SEND FOR UNCLE TOM ON HIS MIGHTY KNEES.
SEND FOR LINCOLN, SEND FOR GRANT.
SEND FOR FREDERICK DOUGLASS, GARRISON, BEECHER,
    LOWELL.
SEND FOR HARRIET TUBMAN, OLD SOJOURNER TRUTH.
SEND FOR MARCUS GARVEY (WHAT?) SUFI (WHO?) FATHER
    DIVINE (WHERE?)
DuBOIS (WHEN?) MALCOLM (OH!) SEND FOR STOKELY. (NO?)
    THEN
SEND FOR ADAM POWELL ON A NON-SUBPOENA DAY.
SEND FOR THE PIED PIPER TO PIPE OUR RATS AWAY.

    (And if nobody comes, send for me.)

2

American Heartbreak

American Heartbreak

I am the American heartbreak—
The rock on which Freedom
Stumped its toe—
The great mistake
That Jamestown made
Long ago.

Ghosts of 1619

Ghosts of all too solid flesh,
Dark ghosts come back to haunt you now,
These dark ghosts to taunt you—
Yet ghosts so solid, ghosts so real
They may not only haunt you—
But rape, rob, steal,
Sit-in, stand-in, stall-in, vote-in
(Even vote for real in Alabam')
And in voting not give a damn
For the fact that white *was* right
Until last night.

Last night?
What happened then?
Flesh-and-blood ghosts
Became flesh-and-blood men?
Got tired of asking, *When?*
Although minority,
Suddenly became majority

(Metaphysically speaking)
In seeking authority?

How can one man be ten?
Or ten be a hundred and ten?
Or a thousand and ten?
Or a million and ten
Are but a thousand and ten
Or a hundred and ten
Or ten—or one—
Or none—
Being ghosts
Of then?

October 16: The Raid

Perhaps
You will remember
John Brown.

John Brown
Who took his gun,
Took twenty-one companions
White and black,
Went to shoot your way to freedom
Where two rivers meet
And the hills of the
South
Look slow at one another—
And died
For your sake.

Now that you are
Many years free,
And the echo of the Civil War

Has passed away,
And Brown himself
Has long been tried at law,
Hanged by the neck,
And buried in the ground—
Since Harpers Ferry
Is alive with ghosts today,
Immortal raiders
Come again to town—

Perhaps
You will recall
John Brown.

Long View: Negro

Emancipation: 1865
Sighted through the
Telescope of dreams
Looms larger,
So much larger,
So it seems,
Than truth can be.

But turn the telescope around,
Look through the larger end—
And wonder why
What was so large
Becomes so small
Again.

Frederick Douglass: 1817–1895

Douglass was someone who,
Had he walked with wary foot
And frightened tread,
From very indecision
Might be dead,
Might have lost his soul,
But instead decided to be bold
And capture every street
On which he set his feet,
To route each path
Toward freedom's goal,
To make each highway
Choose *his* compass' choice,
To all the world cried,
Hear my voice! . . .
Oh, to be a beast, a bird,
Anything but a slave! he said.

Who would be free
Themselves must strike
The first blow, he said.

He died in 1895.
He is not dead.

Still Here

I been scared and battered.
My hopes the wind done scattered.
　Snow has friz me,
　Sun has baked me,
Looks like between 'em they done

Tried to make me
Stop laughin', stop lovin', stop livin'—
But I don't care!
I'm still here!

Words Like Freedom

There are words like *Freedom*
Sweet and wonderful to say.
On my heartstrings freedom sings
All day everyday.

There are words like *Liberty*
That almost make me cry.
If you had known what I know
You would know why.

3

The Bible Belt

Christ in Alabama

Christ is a nigger,
Beaten and black:
Oh, bare your back!

Mary is His mother:
Mammy of the South,
Silence your mouth.

God is His father:
White Master above
Grant Him your love.

Most holy bastard
Of the bleeding mouth,
  Nigger Christ
  On the cross
  Of the South.

Bible Belt

It would be too bad if Jesus
Were to come back black.
There are so many churches
Where he could not pray
In the U.S.A.,
Where entrance to Negroes,
No matter how sanctified,
Is denied,

Where race, not religion,
Is glorified.
But say it—
You may be
Crucified.

Militant

Let all who will
Eat quietly the bread of shame.
I cannot,
Without complaining loud and long,
Tasting its bitterness in my throat,
And feeling to my very soul
It's wrong.
For honest work
You proffer me poor pay,
For honest dreams
Your spit is in my face,
And so my fist is clenched
Today—
To strike your face.

Office Building: Evening

When the white folks get through
   Here come you:

   Got to clean awhile.

When daytime folks
Have made their dough,
   Away they go:

You clean awhile.

When white collars get done,
 You have your "fun"
 Cleaning awhile.

"But just wait, chile . . ."

Florida Road Workers

Hey, Buddy!
Look at me!

I'm makin' a road
For the cars to fly by on,
Makin' a road
Through the palmetto thicket
For light and civilization
To travel on.

I'm makin' a road
For the rich to sweep over
In their big cars
And leave me standin' here.

Sure,
A road helps everybody.
Rich folks ride—
And I get to see 'em ride.
I ain't never seen nobody
Ride so fine before.

Hey, Buddy, look!
I'm makin' a road!

Special Bulletin

Lower the flags
For the dead become alive,
Play hillbilly dirges
That hooded serpents may dance,
Write obituaries
For white-robed warriors
Emerging to the fanfare
Of death rattles.
Muffled drums in Swanee River tempo.
Hand-high salutes—*heil!*
Present arms
With ax handles
Made in Atlanta,
   Sieg
   Heil!
Oh, run, all who have not
Changed your names.
As for you others—
The skin on your black face,
Peel off the skin,
   Peel peel
   Peel off
   The skin.

Mississippi

Oh, what sorrow!
Oh, what pity!
Oh, what pain
That tears and blood
Should mix like rain

And terror come again
To Mississippi.

Again?
Where has terror been?
On vacation? Up North?
In some other section
Of the Nation,
Lying low, unpublicized,
Masked—with only
Jaundiced eyes showing
Through the mask?

What sorrow, pity, pain,
That tears and blood
Still mix like rain
In Mississippi.

Ku Klux

They took me out
To some lonesome place.
They said, "Do you believe
In the great white race?"

I said, "Mister,
To tell you the truth,
I'd believe in anything
If you'd just turn me loose."

The white man said, "Boy,
Can it be
You're a-standin' there
A-sassin' me?"

They hit me in the head
And knocked me down.
And then they kicked me
On the ground.

A klansman said, "Nigger,
Look me in the face—
And tell me you believe in
The great white race."

Justice

That Justice is a blind goddess
Is a thing to which we black are wise:
Her bandage hides two festering sores
That once perhaps were eyes.

Birmingham Sunday

(September 15, 1963)

   Four little girls
Who went to Sunday School that day
And never came back home at all
But left instead
Their blood upon the wall
With spattered flesh
And bloodied Sunday dresses
Torn to shreds by dynamite
That China made aeons ago—
Did not know
That what China made
Before China was ever Red at all

Would redden with their blood
This Birmingham-on-Sunday wall.

   Four tiny girls
Who left their blood upon that wall,
In little graves today await
The dynamite that might ignite
The fuse of centuries of Dragon Kings
Whose tomorrow sings a hymn
The missionaries never taught Chinese
In Christian Sunday School
To implement the Golden Rule.

   Four little girls
Might be awakened someday soon
By songs upon the breeze
As yet unfelt among magnolia trees.

Bombings in Dixie

It's not enough to mourn
And not enough to pray.
Sackcloth and ashes, anyhow,
Save for another day.

The Lord God Himself
Would hardly desire
That men be burned to death—
And bless the fire.

Children's Rhymes

By what sends
the white kids
I ain't sent:
I know I can't
be President.

What don't bug
them white kids
sure bugs me:
We know everybody
ain't free.

Lies written down
for white folks
ain't for us a-tall:
Liberty And Justice—
Huh!—*For All?*

Down Where I Am

Too many years
Beatin' at the door—
I done beat my
Both fists sore.

Too many years
Tryin' to get up there—
Done broke my ankles down,
Got nowhere.

Too many years
Climbin' that hill,

'Bout out of breath.
I got my fill.

I'm gonna plant my feet
On solid ground.
If you want to see me,
Come down.

4

The Face of War

Mother in Wartime

As if it were some noble thing,
She spoke of sons at war,
As if freedom's cause
Were pled anew at some heroic bar,
As if the weapons used today
Killed with great élan,
As if technicolor banners flew
To honor modern man—
Believing everything she read
In the daily news,
(No in-between to choose)
She thought that only
One side won,
Not that *both*
Might lose.

Without Benefit of Declaration

Listen here, Joe,
Don't you know
That tomorrow
You got to go
Out yonder where
The steel winds blow?

Listen here, kid,
It's been said
Tomorrow you'll be dead

Out there where
The rain is lead.

Don't ask me why.
Just go ahead and die.
Hidden from the sky
Out yonder you'll lie:
A medal to your family—
In exchange for
   A guy.

Mama, don't cry.

Official Notice

Dear Death:
I got your message
That my son is dead.
The ink you used
To write it
Is the blood he bled.
You say he died with honor
On the battlefield,
And that I am honored, too,
By this bloody yield.
Your letter
Signed in blood,
With his blood
Is sealed.

Peace

We passed their graves:
The dead men there,
Winners or losers,
Did not care.

In the dark
They could not see
Who had gained
The victory.

Last Prince of the East

Futile of me to offer you my hand,
Last little brown prince
Of Malaysia land.
Your wall is too high
And your moat is too wide—
For the white world's gunboats
Are all on your side.
So you lie in your cradle
And shake your rattle
To the jingo cry
Of blood and battle
While Revolt in the rice fields
Puts on a red gown.

Before you are king,
He'll come to town.

The Dove

. . . and here is
old Picasso and the dove
and dreams as fragile
as pottery with dove
in white on clay
dark brown as
earth is brown
from our old
battle ground . . .

War

The face of war is my face.
The face of war is your face.
   What color
   Is the face
   Of war?
Brown, black, white—
Your face and my face.

Death is the broom
I take in my hands
To sweep the world
   Clean.
I sweep and I sweep
Then mop and I mop.
I dip my broom in blood,
My mop in blood—
And blame you for this,
Because you are *there*,
   Enemy.
It's hard to blame me,

Because I am here—
So I kill you.
And you kill me.
    My name,
Like your name,
    Is war.

5

African Question Mark

Oppression

Now dreams
Are not available
To the dreamers,
Nor songs
To the singers.

In some lands
Dark night
And cold steel
Prevail—
But the dream
Will come back,
And the song
Break
Its jail.

Angola Question Mark

Don't know why I,
Black,
Must still stand
With my back
To the last frontier
Of fear
In my own land.

Don't know why I
Must turn into

A Mau Mau
And lift my hand
Against my fellow man
To live on my own land.

But it is so—
And being so
I know
For you and me
There's
Woe.

Lumumba's Grave

Lumumba was black
And he didn't trust
The whores all powdered
With uranium dust.

Lumumba was black
And he didn't believe
The lies thieves shook
Through their "freedom" sieve.

Lumumba was black.
His blood was red—
And for being a man
They killed him dead.

They buried Lumumba
In an unmarked grave.
But he needs no marker—
For air is his grave.

Sun is his grave,
Moon is, stars are,
Space is his grave.

My heart's his grave,
And it's marked there.
Tomorrow will mark
It everywhere.

Color

Wear it
Like a banner
For the proud—
Not like a shroud.
Wear it
Like a song
Soaring high—
Not moan or cry.

Question and Answer

Durban, Birmingham,
Cape Town, Atlanta,
Johannesburg, Watts,
The earth around
Struggling, fighting,
Dying—for what?

A world to gain.

Groping, hoping,
Waiting—for what?

A world to gain.

Dreams kicked asunder,
Why not go under?

There's a world to gain.

But suppose I don't want it,
Why take it?

To remake it.

History

The past has been a mint
Of blood and sorrow.
That must not be
True of tomorrow.

6

Dinner Guest: Me

Dinner Guest: Me

I know I am
The Negro Problem
Being wined and dined,
Answering the usual questions
That come to white mind
Which seeks demurely
To probe in polite way
The why and wherewithal
Of darkness U.S.A.—
Wondering how things got this way
In current democratic night,
Murmuring gently
Over *fraises du bois,*
"I'm so ashamed of being white."

The lobster is delicious,
The wine divine,
And center of attention
At the damask table, mine.
To be a Problem on
Park Avenue at eight
Is not so bad.
Solutions to the Problem,
Of course, wait.

Northern Liberal

And so
we lick our chops at Birmingham
and say, "See!
Southern dogs have vindicated me—
I knew that this would come."
But who are we to be
so proud that savages
have proven a point
taken late in time
to show how liberal I am?
Above the struggle
I can quite afford to be:
well-fed, degreed,
not beat—elite,
up North.
I send checks,
support your cause,
and lick my chops
at Jim Crow laws
and Birmingham—
where you,
not I
am.

Sweet Words on Race

Sweet words that take
Their own sweet time to flower
And then so quickly wilt
Within the inner ear,
Belie the budding promise
Of their pristine hour

To wither in the
Sultry air of fear.
Sweet words so brave
When danger is not near,
I've heard
So many times before,
I'd just as leave
Not hear them
Anymore.

Un-American Investigators

The committee's fat,
Smug, almost secure
Co-religionists
Shiver with delight
In warm manure
As those investigated—
Too brave to name a name—
Have pseudonyms revealed
In Gentile game
   Of who,
   Born Jew,
   Is who?
Is not your name Lipshitz?
   Yes.
Did you not change it
For subversive purposes?
   No.
For nefarious gain?
   Not so.
Are you sure?
The committee shivers

With delight in
Its manure.

Slave

To ride piggy-back
to the market of death
there to purchase a slave,
a slave who died young,
having given up breath—
unwittingly,
of course—
a slave who died young,
perhaps from a fix
with a rusty needle
infected,
to purchase a slave
to the market of death
I ride protected.

Undertow

The solid citizens
Of the country club set,
Caught between
Selma and Peking,
Feel the rug of dividends,
Bathmats of pride,
Even soggy country club
Pink paper towels
Dropped on the MEN'S ROOM floor
Slipping out from under them
Like waves of sea

Between Selma, Peking,
Westchester
And me.

Little Song on Housing

Here I come!
Been saving all my life
To get a nice home
For me and my wife.

White folks flee—
As soon as you see
My problems
And me!

Neighborhood's clean,
But the house is old,
Prices are doubled
When I get sold:
Still I buy.

White folks fly—
Soon as you spy
My wife
And I!

Next thing you know,
Our neighbors all colored are.
The candy store's
Turned into a bar:
White folks have left
The whole neighborhood
To my black self.

White folks, flee!
Still—there is me!
White folks, fly!
Here am I!

Cultural Exchange

In the Quarter of the Negroes
Where the doors are doors of paper
Dust of dingy atoms
Blows a scratchy sound.
Amorphous jack-o'-lanterns caper
and the wind won't wait for midnight
For fun to blow doors down.

By the river and the railroad
With fluid far-off going
Boundaries bind unbinding
A whirl of whistles blowing.
No trains or steamboats going—
Yet Leontyne's unpacking.

In the Quarter of the Negroes
Where the doorknob lets in Lieder
More than German ever bore,
Her yesterday past grandpa—
Not of her own doing—
In a pot of collard greens
Is gently stewing.

Pushcarts fold and unfold
In a supermarket sea.
And we better find out, mama,
Where is the colored laundromat
Since we moved up to Mount Vernon.

In the pot behind the paper doors
On the old iron stove what's cooking?
What's smelling, Leontyne?
Lieder, lovely Lieder
And a leaf of collard green.
Lovely Lieder, Leontyne.

You know, right at Christmas
They asked me if my blackness,
Would it rub off?
I said, *Ask your mama.*

Dreams and nightmares!
Nightmares, dreams, oh!
Dreaming that the Negroes
Of the South have taken over—
Voted all the Dixiecrats
Right out of power—
Comes the COLORED HOUR:
Martin Luther King is Governor of Georgia,
Dr. Rufus Clement his Chief Adviser,
A. Philip Randolph the High Grand Worthy.
In white pillared mansions
Sitting on their wide verandas,
Wealthy Negroes have white servants,
White sharecroppers work the black plantations,
And colored children have white mammies:
   Mammy Faubus
   Mammy Eastland
   Mammy Wallace
Dear, dear darling old white mammies—
Sometimes even buried with our family.
   Dear old
   Mammy Faubus!
Culture, they say, *is a two-way street:*

Hand me my mint julep, mammy.
  Hurry up!
  Make haste!

Frosting

Freedom
Is just frosting
On somebody else's
Cake—
And so must be
Till we
Learn how to
Bake.

Impasse

I could tell you,
If I wanted to,
What makes me
What I am.

But I don't
Really want to—
And you don't
Give a damn.

7

Daybreak in Alabama

Freedom

Freedom will not come
Today, this year
   Nor ever
Through compromise and fear.

I have as much right
As the other fellow has
   To stand
On my two feet
And own the land.

I tire so of hearing people say,
Let things take their course.
Tomorrow is another day.
I do not need my freedom when I'm dead.
I cannot live on tomorrow's bread.
   Freedom
   Is a strong seed
   Planted
   In a great need.
   I live here, too.
   I want freedom
   Just as you.

Go Slow

Go *slow*, they say—
While the bite
Of the dog is fast.
Go *slow*, I hear—
While they tell me
You can't eat here!
You can't live here!
You can't work here!
Don't demonstrate! Wait!—
While they lock the gate.

Am I supposed to be God,
Or an angel with wings
And a halo on my head
While jobless I starve dead?
Am I supposed to forgive
And meekly live
Going slow, slow, slow,
Slow, slow, slow,
Slow, slow,
Slow,
Slow,
Slow?
????
???
??
?

Merry-Go-Round

Colored child
at carnival

Where is the Jim Crow section
On this merry-go-round,
Mister, cause I want to ride?
Down South where I come from
White and colored
Can't sit side by side.
Down South on the train
There's a Jim Crow car.
On the bus we're put in the back—
But there ain't no back
To a merry-go-round!
Where's the horse
For a kid that's black?

Dream Dust

Gather out of star-dust
   Earth-dust,
   Cloud-dust,
And splinters of hail,
One handful of dream-dust
   Not for sale.

Stokely Malcolm Me

i have been seeking
what i have never found
what i don't know what i want

but it must be around
i been upset
since the day before last
but that day was so long
i done forgot when it passed
yes almost forgot
what i have not found
but i know it must be
somewhere around.

you live in the Bronx
so folks say.

Stokely,
did i ever live
up your
way?
???
??
?

Slum Dreams

Little dreams
Of springtime
Bud in sunny air
With no roots
To nourish them,
Since no stems
Are there—
Detached,
Naïve,
So young,
On air alone
They're hung.

Georgia Dusk

Sometimes there's a wind in the Georgia dusk
That cries and cries and cries
In lonely pity through the Georgia dusk
Veiling what the darkness hides.

Sometimes there's blood in the Georgia dusk
Left by a streak of sun,
A crimson trickle in the Georgia dusk.
Whose blood? . . . Everyone's.

Sometimes a wind in the Georgia dusk
Scatters hate like seed
To sprout their bitter barriers
Where the sunsets bleed.

Where? When? Which?

When the cold comes
With a bitter fragrance
Like rusty iron and mint,
And the wind blows
Sharp as integration
With an edge like apartheid,
And it is winter,
And the cousins of the too-thin suits
Ride on bitless horses
Tethered by something worse than pride,
Which areaway, or bar,
Or station waiting room
Will not say,
Horse and horseman, outside!
With old and not too gentle
Apartheid?

Vari-Colored Song

If I had a heart of gold,
As have some folks I know,
I'd up and sell my heart of gold
And head North with the dough.

But I don't have a heart of gold.
My heart's not even lead.
It's made of plain old Georgia clay.
That's why my heart is red.

I wonder why red clay's so red
And Georgia skies so blue.
I wonder why it's *yes* to me,
But *yes, sir,* sir, to you.

I wonder why the sky's so blue
And why the clay's so red.
Why down South is always *down,*
And never *up* instead.

Jim Crow Car

Get out the lunch-box of your dreams
And bite into the sandwich of your heart,
And ride the Jim Crow car until it screams
And, like an atom bomb, bursts apart.

Warning

Negroes,
Sweet and docile,
Meek, humble, and kind:

Beware the day
They change their mind!

Wind
In the cotton fields,
Gentle breeze:
Beware the hour
It uproots trees!

Daybreak in Alabama

When I get to be a composer
I'm gonna write me some music about
Daybreak in Alabama
And I'm gonna put the purtiest songs in it
Rising out of the ground like a swamp mist
And falling out of heaven like soft dew.
I'm gonna put some tall tall trees in it
And the scent of pine needles
And the smell of red clay after rain
And long red necks
And poppy colored faces
And big brown arms
And the field daisy eyes
Of black and white black white black people
And I'm gonna put white hands
And black hands and brown and yellow hands
And red clay earth hands in it
Touching everybody with kind fingers
And touching each other natural as dew
In that dawn of music when I
Get to be a composer
And write about daybreak
In Alabama.

Uncollected Poems

1951–1960

Prelude to Our Age

A Negro History Poem

History's long page
Records the whole vast
Prelude to our age.

Across the chapters
Of recorded time
Shadows of so many hands
Have fallen,
Among them mine:
   Negro.

At first only
The spoken word of bard or chief,
And the beaten drum
That carried instant history
Across the night,
Or linked man with the mystery
Of powers beyond sight.
Pictures on stone, hieroglyphics,
Parchment, illuminated scrolls.

   Homer's
   "Blameless Ethiopians."

On all these rolls landmarking man,
The shadow of my hand:
   Negro.

Aesop, Antar, Terence,
Various Pharaohs,
Sheba, too.
Ethiopia, Ghana, Songhay.
Arab and African; the Moors

Gave Spain her castanets
And Senegal her prayers.

All this before the type that moved
in which Juan Latino spoke:
"Ad Catholicum-Pariter et Invictissimum"—
The shadow of my hand
Across the printed word:
 Granada, 1573.

 Yoruba, Benin, Guinea,
 Timbuctoo and Abderrahman Sadi's
 "Tarikh es Soudan."

Meanwhile Jamestown links its chains
Between the Gold Coast and our land.
 Jamestown, Virginia, 1619.

But lately dead Elizabeth the Queen.
But lately come to throne,
King James, whose Bible is our own.
As Sadi chronicles his great
 "Tarikh es Soudan,"
With Africa a link of chains connects our land.
Caught in those chains, my hand:
 Negro.

Yet Boston's Phillis Wheatley, slave, wrote her poems,
And Washington, the general, praised—
Washington who righted wrong—
But those of us who had no rights
 made an unwritten song:

 Go down, Moses,
 Way down in Egypt land,
 And tell old Pharaoh
 To let my people go. . . .

Black Crispus Attucks died
That our land might be free.
  His death
  Did not free me.
When Banneker made his almanac
  I was not free.
When Toussaint freed the blacks of Haiti,
  I was not free.

In other lands Dumas and Pushkin wrote—
  But we,
  Who could not write, made songs:

  Swing low, sweet chariot,
  Coming for to carry me home . . .
  Oh, I looked over Jordan
  And what did I see—

Phillis, Crispus, Toussaint,
Banneker, Dumas, Pushkin,
All of these were me—
  Not free:

  As long as one
  Man is in chains,
  No man is free.

Yet Ira Aldridge played Shakespeare in London.
Frederick Douglass ran away to freedom,
Wrote books, made speeches, edited "The North Star."
Sojourner Truth made speeches, too.
Harriet Tubman led her marches.
"Uncle Tom's Cabin" swept the nation—
While we, who were not free and could not write a word,
Gave freedom a song the whole earth heard:

  Oh, Freedom!

Freedom over me!
Before I'd be a slave
I'd be buried in my grave
And go home to my Lord
And be free.

Nat Turner, Denmark Vesey
And thousands nameless went home.
Black men died at Harpers Ferry with John Brown.
Lovejoy, Garrison, Wendell Phillips spoke.
The North star guided men along the Quaker underground
To Canada—hills to cross, rivers to ford.
Sermons, revolt, prayers, Civil War—

Mine eyes have seen the glory
Of the coming of the Lord!

Lincoln:
1863.
Once slaves—
"Henceforth and forever free."

My Lord, what a morning,
My Lord, what a morning,
My Lord, what a morning,
When the stars began to fall!

Booker T.—
A school, Tuskegee.
Paul Laurence Dunbar—
A poem, a song, a "Lindy Lou."
Fisk University and its Jubilees.
Black Congressmen of Reconstruction days.
Black comics with their minstrel ways,
Then Williams & Walker, "In Dahomey," "Bandana Land"
Ragtime sets the pattern for a nation's songs

And Handy writes the blues
   For me—
   Now free.

Free to build my churches and my schools—
   Mary McLeod Bethune.
Free to explore clay and sweet potatoes—
   Dr. Carver.
Free to take our songs across the world—
   Anderson, Maynor, Robeson,
   Josephine Baker, Florence Mills,
Free to sit in councils of the nation—
   Johnson, Hastie, Dawson, Powell.
Free to make blood plasma—
   Charles R. Drew.
Free to move at will in great migrations
South to North across the nation—
Savannah to Sugar Hill,
Rampart Street to Paradise Valley,
Yamakraw to Yale.
Free to fight in wars as others do—
   Free—yet segregated.

   As man or soldier
   Underrated.

The 10th Cavalry at San Juan Hill:
   "As I heard one of the Rough Riders say,"
   Wrote Theodore Roosevelt,
   " 'They can drink out of our canteens.' "

The 369th Infantry at Champagne:
   To Henry Johnson
   And to Needham Roberts,
   The *Croix de Guerre.*

The 332nd Fighter Group over the Mediterranean:
    To more than eighty pilots,
    The Distinguished Flying Cross.

In the Pacific the Navy Cross to Dorie Miller.
    Me, hero and killer.
    (Yet segregated.)

    Me, peacemaker, too—
    Ralph Bunche
    Between the Arab
    And the Jew.

Du Bois, Woodson, Johnson, Frazier,
Robert S. Abbott, T. Thomas Fortune,
"The Afro-American," "The Black Dispatch."
All the time the written record grows—
"The Crisis," "Phylon," "Opportunity,"
Schomburg, McKay, Cullen, "Native Son,"
Papers, stories, poems the whole world knows—
The ever growing history of man
Shadowed by my hand:
    Negro.

Other hands whose fingers intertwine
With mine tell our story, too:
Park, Myrdal, Sinclair Lewis,
Smith, Van Vechten, Bucklin Moon.
Surveys, novels, movies, plays
That trace the maze of patterns
Woven by democracy and me,
    Now free.

And all the while
The rising power of my vote
Helping build democracy—

My vote, my labor, lodges, clubs,
My N.A.A.C.P.—
 The National Association
 For The Advancement
 Of Colored People—
 All the way from a Jim Crow dining car
To the United States Supreme Court—
For the right to get a meal on a train.

All the way from a Jim Crow school
To the United States Supreme Court—
For the right to equal education.

All the way from ghetto covenants
To the United States Supreme Court—
For the right to housing free from segregation.

Thus I help to build democracy
For our nation.
Thus by decree across the history of our land—
The shadow of my hand:
 Negro

 All this
 A prelude to our age:
 Today.

Tomorrow
Is another
Page.

Where Service Is Needed

For the Negro Nurse there's been no easy way.
The bars have been high, the day a long day
When the hand that could tend the sick or the hurt
Must also combat Jim Crow's dirt.

No caution, no gloves, no antiseptic, no mask
Could protect her from prejudice as she stuck to her task.
Only devotion, and the will to be what she set out to be,
Kept the Negro nurse on her road to today's victory.

From America's garden now
The ugly weeds are being weeded:
Only five states bar their doors to dark hands
That would serve where service is needed.

In the Army, the Navy, colored nurses attend.
Her long gallant struggle portends a good end.
"Negro nurse" is a phrase men no longer need say.
"American nurse" means all nurses today.

The bars have been high. There is no magic wand;
Only unity and faith have brought this new dawn
Where the rights of democracy to all are ceded:
Her skilled hands may serve where service is needed.

Consider Me

Consider me,
A colored boy,
Once sixteen,
Once five, once three,
Once nobody,

Now me.
Before me
Papa, mama,
Grandpa, grandma,
So on back
To original
Pa.

   (A capital letter there,
   He
   Being Mystery.)

Consider me,
Colored boy,
Downtown at eight,
Sometimes working late,
Overtime pay
To sport away,
Or save,
Or give my Sugar
For the things
She needs.

My Sugar,
Consider her
Who works, too—
Has to.
One don't make enough
For all the stuff
It takes to live.
Forgive me
What I lack,
Black,
Caught in a crack
That splits the world in two

From China
By way of Arkansas
To Lenox Avenue.

Consider me,
On Friday the eagle flies.
Saturday laughter, a bar, a bed.
Sunday prayers syncopate glory.
Monday comes,
To work at eight,
Late,
Maybe.

Consider me,
Descended also
From the
Mystery.

So Long

So long
is in the song
and it's in the way you're gone
but it's like a foreign language
in my mind
and maybe was I blind
I could not see
and would not know
you're gone so long
so long.

Tomorrow's Seed

Proud banner of death,
I see them waving
There against the sky,
Struck deep in Spanish earth
Where your dark bodies lie
Inert and helpless—
So they think
Who do not know
That from your death
New life will grow.
For there are those who cannot see
The mighty roots of liberty
Push upward in the dark
To burst in flame—
A million stars—
And one your name:
    Man
Who fell in Spanish earth:
Human seed
For freedom's birth.

Hero—International Brigade

Blood,
Or a flag,
Or a flame
Or life itself
Are they the same:
Our dream?
    I came.
An ocean in-between
And half a continent.

Frontiers,
And mountains skyline tall,
And governments that told me NO,
YOU CANNOT GO!
    I came.
On tomorrow's bright frontiers
I placed the strength and wisdom
Of my years.
Not much,
For I am young.
(*Was* young,
Perhaps it's better said—
For now I'm dead.)

But had I lived four score and ten
Life could not've had
A better end.
I've given what I wished
And what I had to give
That others live.
And when the bullets
Cut my heart away,
And the blood
Gushed to my throat
I wondered if it were blood
Gushing there.
Or a red flame?
Or just my death
Turned into life?
They're all the same:
Our dream!
    My death!
    Your life!
    Our blood!

One flame!
They're all the same!

The Christmas Story

Tell me again the Christmas story:
Christ is born in all His glory!

Baby born in Manger dark
Lighting ages with the spark
Of innocence that is the Child
Trusting all within His smile.

Tell again the Christmas story
With the halo of His glory:
Halo born of humbleness
By the breath of cattle blest,
By the poverty of stall
Where a bed of straw is all,
By a door closed at the Inn,
Only men of means get in
By a door closed to the poor,
Christ is born on earthen floor
In a stable with no lock—
Yet kingdoms tremble at the shock
Of a King in swaddling clothes
At an address no one knows
Because there is no painted sign—
Nothing but a star divine,
Nothing but a halo bright
About His young head in the night,
Nothing but the wondrous light
Of innocence that is the Child

Trusting all within His smile.

Mary's Son of golden star:
Wise Men journey from afar.
Mary's Son in Manger born:
Music of the Angel's horn.
Mary's Son in straw and glory:

Wonder of the Christmas story!

No Regrets

Out of love,
No regrets—
Though the goodness
Be wasted forever.

Out of love,
No regrets—
Though the return
Be never.

A Ballad of Negro History

(So Much to Write About)

Written especially for The Authors Association at the request of Dr. M.
A. Majors, June, 1951.

There is so much to write about
In the Negro race.
On each page of history
Glows a dusky face.
Ancient Pharaohs come to mind
Away back in B.C.

Ethiopia's jewelled hand
Writes a scroll for me.
It was a black man bore the Cross
For Christ at Calvary.
There is so much to write about
In the Negro race.
Though now of Ghana's Empire
There remains no trace,
Once Africa's great cultures
Lighted Europe's dark
As Mandingo and Songhay
Cradled learning's ark
Before the Moors crossed into Spain
To leave their mark.
There is so much to write about
In the Negro race.
Ere the ships of slavery sailed
The seas of dark disgrace,
Once Antar added
Winged words to poetry's lore
And Juan Latino searched
The medieval heart's deep core—
All this before black men in chains
At Jamestown were put ashore.
There is so much to write about
In the Negro race,
So many thrilling stories
Time cannot erase:
Crispus Attucks' blow for freedom,
Denmark Vesey's, too.
Sojourner Truth, Fred Douglass,
And the heroes John Brown knew—
Before the Union Armies gave
Black men proud uniforms of blue.
1863—Emancipation!

The Negro race
Began its mighty struggle
For a rightful place
In the making of America
To whose young land it gave
Booker T. and Carver—
Each genius born a slave—
Yet foreordained to greatness
On the crest of freedom's wave.
Paul Laurence Dunbar
Penned his rhymes of lyric lace—
All the sadness and the humor
Of the Negro race.
To the words of colored Congressmen
The Halls of Congress rang.
Handy wrote the blues.
Williams and Walker sang.
Still on southern trees today
Dark bodies hang.
The story is one of struggle
For the Negro race—
But in spite of all the lynch ropes,
We've marched on to take our place:
Woodson, Negro History Week,
Du Bois, Johnson, Drew,
Cullen, Maynor, Bunche,
The cultural record grew.
Edith Sampson went around the world
To tell the nations what she knew—
And Josephine came home from France
To claim an equal chance
Through song and dance.
There is so much to write about
To sing about, to shout about
In the Negro race!

On each page of history
America sees my face—
On each page of history
We leave a shining trace—
On each page of history
   My race!
     My race!
       My race!

Hope for Harlem

There's a new skyline in Harlem,
It's tall and proud and fine.
At night its walls are gleaming
Where a thousand windows shine.

There's a new skyline in Harlem
That belongs to you and me
As the dark old ugly houses
Tumble into memory—

Memory of those dingy stairs,
Memory of my helpless prayers,
Memory of the landlord's stares
When you asked him for a few repairs.

Now there's a new skyline in Harlem
It's rising tall and free—
And if it keeps on rising
There'll be a brand new *me*.

Don't you know it makes a difference
When you got a clean new house?
I used to hear those old rats gnawing.
Now I don't even hear a mouse.

I used to climb those old steps,
Up dark old creaking stairs—
And sometimes I said a cuss word
Before I said my prayers.

But there's a new skyline in Harlem,
And I'm thankful when I pray
That the yard is bigger than a park,
And kids have a chance to play.

That the walls are painted pretty,
And the bathroom has a shower—
For folks who never thought they'd live
In a house that's got a tower.

> *A stone to throw*
> *Or a stone to build with?*
> *A brick for a brickbat*
> *Or a brick for a wall?*
> *Stones are better*
> *For building,*
> *Bricks are better*
> *For a wall.*

That's why I'm mighty happy
When I see those old walls fall,
When I see dead trees uprooted
For new trees to grow tall.

And I'm mighty glad I'm lucky
My name stayed on the list
To get a new apartment
Where I *live*—not just exist.

But I can't forget my brothers
Nor my sisters down the street

In those broken down old houses
Where both ends never meet.

Houses where the steps are creaking,
Where rats gnaw at the floors,
And a dozen names are sticking
In the doorbells at the doors.

Where clean clothes hang like banners
From dingy wall to wall—
Clothes that are *really* banners
Waving for us all—

Waving to the glory
Of those who climb the stairs
To wash the clothes of trying
In the soapsuds of their prayers.

But the old skyline is sagging.
It looks sadder than before.
So I hope the day is coming
When there won't be any more.

Houses where the steps are creaking
And rats gnaw at the floors
And a dozen names are sticking
In each doorbell at the doors.

For there's a new skyline in Harlem.
It's rising here and there.
We're waiting for that skyline
To start rising everywhere!

A new skyline in Harlem—
The answer to a prayer!

Ultimatum: Kid to Kid

Go home, stupid,
And wash your dirty face.
Go home, stupid,
This is not your place.

Go home, stupid,
You don't belong here.
If you don't go,
I will pull your ear.

I ask you if you'd like to play.
"Huh?" is all you know to say,
Standing 'round here
In the way.

So go home, stupid!
I'll spit in your eye!
Stupid, go home—
Before I cry.

Ballad of the Two Thieves

When Jesus died at Calvary
For what our world believes,
On either side upon a Cross
They hung two thieves—

Two members of a lowly mob
Who stole to get their bread
Were tied upon a Cross that day
To taste of death instead.

One thief looked at Christ and said,
If you're so great
As your followers swear—
Save yourself! Save me!
And save my brother thief there—
If you're as great
As your followers swear!

But he did not speak for his brother thief
Hanging on the gallows tree,
For the other thief cried only,
Lord, remember me!

Christ had the thorns upon His head
And in His mouth was gall.
From His palms the blood ran red
And on the ground did fall.

For the sins of man I suffer.
For the sins of man I die—
My body and my blood
Are the answer to your cry.

In the garden one betrayed me,
And Peter denied me thrice
But you who cry, Remember me!
Go with me to Paradise.

Africa

Sleepy giant,
You've been resting awhile.
Now I see the thunder
And the lightning
In your smile.

Now I see
The storm clouds
In your waking eyes:
The thunder,
The wonder,
And the young
Surprise.
Your every step reveals
The new stride
In your thighs.

Envoy to Africa

My name is Lord Piggly-Wiggly Wogglesfoot Brown.
I was born in a quaint old English manor town.
I now find myself engaged in a diplomatic chore
That looks as though it might turn into a bit of a bore.
I was sent to inform the natives of this dark place
That the Atlantic Charter will eventually apply to their race.
Of course, at the moment, we could hardly afford
To stretch the Atlantic Charter that broad.
But I will say this to each native race:
  Some day you'll be equal
  If you'll just stay in your place.

Ballad of Booker T.

Booker T.
Was a practical man.
He said, Till the soil
And learn from the land.
Let down your bucket
Where you are.

Your fate is here,
Not afar.
To help yourself
And your fellow man,
Train your head,
Your heart, and your hand.
For smartness alone
Is surely not meet—
If you haven't
At the same time
Got something to eat.
At Tuskegee
He built a school
With book-learning there
Plus the workman's tool.
He started out
In a simple way—
For yesterday
Was not today.
Sometimes he had
Compromise in his talk—
A man must crawl
Before he can walk:
In Alabama in '85
A Negro was lucky
To be alive.
But Booker T.
Was nobody's fool:
You may carve a dream
With a humble tool.
The tallest tower
Can tumble down
If it is not rooted
In solid ground.
So, being a far-seeing

Practical man,
He said, Train your head,
Your heart, and your hand.
Your fate is here,
Not afar,
Let down your bucket
Where you are.

Addition

Put 5 and 5 together
And see if it makes 10.

It does—
If 5 is exactly 5.

But don't let women
Come between—
Or men.

Poet to Bigot

I have done so little
For you,
And you have done so little
For me,
That we have good reason
Never to agree.

I, however,
Have such meagre
Power,
Clutching at a
Moment,

While you control
An hour.

But your hour is
A stone.

My moment is
A flower.

Room

Each little room
Should be
Protective and alone
When there are two—
But wide open
To the air
When only one
Is there.

Do You Reckon?

Mr. White Man, White Man,
How can it be,
You sleep with my sister,
Yet you won't shake hands with me?

Miss White Lady, Lady,
Tell me, if you can,
Why you hard-work my mother,
Yet take my brother for your man?

White Man, White Lady,
What's your story, anyway?

You love me in the night time
And hate me in the day.

Dixie, Dixie, Dixie,
What make you do me like you do?
But I guess if I was white
I would act the same way, too.

Lincoln University: 1954

This is the dream grown young
By but a hundred years,
The dream so bravely tended
Through a century of fears,
The dream so gently nourished
By a century of tears—
The dream grown ever younger,
Greener, fresher
Through the years of working,
Praying, striving, learning,
The dream become a beacon
Brightly burning.

Draftees

Leave your Coras
And your Oras
In the candy stores
And the cocktail bars.

Leave your papas
And your mamas
And your sisters

And your brothers
And your cousins
By the dozens
Behind.

Take your little bag
With a toothbrush and a comb
And leave home.

What's on your mind?

Goodbye, Ora!
Goodbye, Cora!
Goodbye, Kiddie!

Hello, Biddie,
Overseas.

Basic training
(That is basic)
Is basic
In these.

Azikiwe in Jail

The British said to Azikiwe,
We're tired of you running around loose.
We're going to grab you—
And cook your goose.

Azikiwe said to the British,
That may be—
But you'll have a tough goose
If you cook me!

Old Walt

Old Walt Whitman
Went finding and seeking,
Finding less than sought
Seeking more than found,
Every detail minding
Of the seeking or the finding.

Pleasured equally
In seeking as in finding,
Each detail minding,
Old Walt went seeking
And finding.

Us: Colored

So strange,
We are completely out of range—
Becomes a cause
Beyond the laws—
So strange.

Miss Blues'es Child

If the blues would let me,
Lord knows I would smile.
If the blues would let me,
I would smile, smile, smile.
Instead of that I'm cryin'—
I must be Miss Blues'es child.

You were my moon up in the sky,
At night my wishing star.
I love you, oh, I love you so—
But you have gone so far!

Now my days are lonely.
And night-time drives me wild.
In my heart I'm crying,
I'm just Miss Blues'es child!

Delinquent

Little Julie
Has grown quite tall.
Folks say she don't like
To stay home at all.

Little Julie
Has grown quite stout.
Folks say it's not just
Stomach sticking out.

Little Julie
Has grown quite wise—
A tiger, a lion, and an owl
In her eyes.

Little Julie
Says she don't care!
What she means is:
Nobody cares
Anywhere.

Mean Old Yesterday

That mean old yesterday
Keeps on following me.
The things I've said and done
Haunt me like a misery.

What I did last year—
How come it matters still today?
The snow that fell last winter's
Melted away.

I thought you'd done forgotten
What happened way last week,
But when I saw you this morning,
You turned your head and would not speak.

Memory like an elephant,
Never forget a thing!
Well, if you feel like that, baby,
Gimme back my diamond ring.

In Explanation of Our Times

The folks with no titles in front of their names
all over the world
are raring up and talking back
to the folks called Mister.

You say you thought everybody was called Mister?

No, son, not everybody.
In Dixie, often they won't call Negroes Mister.
In China before what happened
They had no intention of calling coolies Mister.

Dixie to Singapore, Cape Town to Hong Kong
the Misters won't call lots of other folks Mister.
They call them, Hey George!
   Here, Sallie!
   Listen, Coolie!
   Hurry up, Boy!
   And things like that.

George Sallie Coolie Boy gets tired sometimes.
So all over the world today
folks with not even Mister in front of their names
are raring up and talking back
to those called Mister.
From Harlem past Hong Kong talking back.

Shut up, says Gerald L. K. Smith.
Shut up, says the Governor of South Carolina.
Shut up, says the Governor of Singapore.
Shut up, says Strydom.

Hell no shut up! say the people
with no titles in front of their names.
Hell, no! It's time to talk back now!
History says it's time,
And the radio, too, foggy with propaganda
that says a mouthful
and don't mean half it says—
but is true anyhow:
   LIBERTY!
   FREEDOM!
   DEMOCRACY!
True anyhow no matter how many
Liars use those words.

The people with no titles in front of their names
hear those words and shout them back

at the Misters, Lords, Generals, Viceroys,
Governors of South Carolina, Gerald L. K. Strydoms.

> Shut up, people!
> Shut up! Shut up!
> Shut up, George!
> Shut up, Sallie!
> Shut up, Coolie!
> Shut up, Indian!
> Shut up, Boy!

George Sallie Coolie Indian Boy
black brown yellow bent down working
earning riches for the whole world
with no title in front of name
just man woman tired says:

> No shut up!
> Hell no shut up!
> So, naturally, there's trouble
> in these our times
> because of people with no titles
> in front of their names.

Plaint

Money and art
Are far apart

The Thorn

Now there will be nobody, you say,
To start a *cause célèbre,*
To snatch a brand from the burning,
Or be a thorn in the side.

You must be forgetting
The cause not yet célèbre,
The brand that's in the burning,
The thorn that awaits turning—
That turns with nobody there
To start the turning.

Brotherly Love
A Little Letter to the White
Citizens of the South

In line of what my folks say in Montgomery,
In line of what they're teaching about love,
When I reach out my hand, will *you* take it—
Or cut it off and leave a nub above?

If I found it in my heart to love you,
And if I thought I really could,
If I said, "Brother, I forgive you,"
I wonder, would it do *you* any good?

So long, so *long* a time you've been calling
Me *all* kinds of names, pushing me down—
I been swimming with my head deep under water,
And you wished I would stay under till I drown.

But I didn't! I'm still swimming! Now you're mad
Because I won't ride in the back end of your bus.

When I answer, "Anyhow, I'm gonna love you,"
Still and yet *you* want to make a fuss.

Now listen, white folks!
In line with Reverend King down in Montgomery—
Also because the Bible says I must—
I'm gonna love you—*yes, I will! Or BUST!*

Two Somewhat Different Epigrams

I
Oh, God of dust and rainbows, help us see
That without dust the rainbow would not be.

II
I look with awe upon the human race
And God, who sometimes spits right in its face.

Last Call

I look out into the Yonder—
And I don't know where I go—
So I cry, *Lord! Lord!*

Yours is the only name I know.

Some folks might say Your ear is deaf
To one who never called before.
Some folks might say You'll scorn me
Since I never sought Your door.

Yet I cry, *Lord! Lord!*

Lord, that is Your name?

I never knew You,
Never called You.
Still I call You now.

I'm game.

Late Corner

The street light
On its lonely arm
Becomes
An extension
Of the Cross—
The Cross itself
A lonely arm
Whose light is lost.

Oh, lonely world!
Oh, lonely light!
Oh, lonely Cross!

Acceptance

God, in His infinite wisdom
Did not make me very wise—
So when my actions are stupid
They hardly take God by surprise.

Testament

What shall I leave my son
When I am dead and gone?
    Room in hell to join me
    When he passes on.
What shall I leave my daughter,
The apple of my eye?
    A thousand pounds of salt
    For tears if she should cry.
What shall I leave my wife
Who nagged me to my death?
    I'll leave her more to nag about
    Than she's got breath.

Gone Boy

Playboy of the dawn,
Solid gone!
Out all night
Until 12—1—2 a.m.

Next day
When he should be gone
To work—
Dog-gone!
He ain't gone.

Memo to Non-White Peoples

They will let you have dope
Because they are quite willing
To drug you or kill you.

They will let you have babies
Because they are quite willing
To pauperize you—
Or use your kids as labor boys
For army, air force, or uranium mine.

They will let you have alcohol
To make you sodden and drunk
And foolish.

They will gleefully let you
Kill your damn self any way you choose
With liquor, drugs, or whatever.

It's the same from Cairo to Chicago,
Cape Town to the Caribbean,
Do you travel the Stork Club circuit
To dear old Shepherd's Hotel?
(Somebody burnt Shepherd's up.)
I'm sorry but it is
The same from Cairo to Chicago,
Cape Town to the Carib Hilton,
Exactly the same.

Expendable

We will take you and kill you,
Expendable.

We will fill you full of lead,
Expendable.

And when you are dead
In the nice cold ground,

We'll put your name
above your head—

If your head
Can be found.

Bouquet

Gather quickly
Out of darkness
All the songs you know
And throw them at the sun
Before they melt
Like snow.

Departure

She lived out a decent span of years
And went to death as should a queen,
Regal in her bravery, hiding fears
More generous than mean—
    Yet even these,
    Lest loved ones weep,
    She carried hidden
    In her heart
    To sleep.

Dixie South Africa

All the craziness
Of your craziness—
Is an Alka-Seltzer tablet

In the late-night glass of the world:
Watch it melt away
In the dew
Of day.

Communiqué

I'm sorry for you
Sitting in the driver's seat
With bebop hands
And ragtime feet.
It would indeed
Be good news
Could you but learn
To sing a blues
Or play a boogie-
Woogie beat
So heart might leap
To head or feet.
It is too bad,
Indeed it's sad,
With all the culture
That you've had,
At this late date
Your rhythms don't
Coordinate.
I'm sorry, man!
With all the billing
That you've got,
You're still
Not so hot.

Casual

Death don't ring no doorbells.
Death don't knock.
Death don't bother to open no doors,
Just comes on through the walls like TV,
Like King Cole on the radio, cool. . . .

Next thing you know, Death's there.
You don't know where Death came from:
Death just comes in
And don't ring no bell.

Numbered

I think my days are numbered.
I think my days are few.
I think my days are numbered,
Baby, yes, I do!

Which is the reason
I spend my nights with you.

The Last Man Living

When the last man living
Is left alive on earth,
And somebody knocks at the door—
If I am the last man living
I will be no more!

Who's that? No answer.
Who is that, I say?
If you don't intend to answer,

Then—just—go—away.

Might you be human—
Or might you be a ghost?
Or can you be myself
Imagining things, at most?

If you're somebody else,
And I'm the last man left alive,
Just get on away from here—
'Cause I don't want no jive!

On a Pallet of Straw

They did not travel in an airplane.
They did not travel by car.
They did not travel on a streamline train.
They traveled on foot from afar.
They traveled on foot from afar.
They did not seek for a fine hotel,
They did not seek an inn,
They did not seek a bright motel,
They sought a cattle bin.
They sought a cattle bin.
Who were these travelers on the road?
And where were they going? And why?
They were Three Wise Men who came from the East,
And they followed a star in the sky,
A star in the sky.
What did they find when they got to the barn?
What did they find near the stall?
What did they find on a pallet of straw?
They found there the Lord of all!
They found the Lord of all!

Carol of the Brown King

Of the three Wise Men
Who came to the King,
One was a brown man,
So they sing.
Of the three Wise Men
Who followed the Star,
One was a brown king
From afar.
They brought fine gifts
Of spices and gold
In jeweled boxes
Of beauty untold.
Unto His humble
Manger they came
And bowed their heads
In Jesus' name.
Three Wise Men,
One dark like me—
Part of His
Nativity.

On a Christmas Night

In Bethlehem on a Christmas night
All around the Child shone a holy light.
All around His head was a halo bright
On a Christmas night.
"We have no room," the innkeeper called,
So the glory fell where the cows were stalled,
But among the guests were Three Kings who called
On a Christmas night.
How can it be such a light shines here

In this humble stable once cold and drear?
Oh, the Child has come to bring good cheer
On a Christmas night!
And what is the name of the little One?
His name is Jesus—He's God's own Son.
Be happy, happy, everyone
On a Christmas night!

Ballad of Mary's Son

It was in the Spring.
The Passover had come.
There was fasting in the streets and joy.
But an awful thing
Happened in the Spring—
Men who knew not what they did
Killed Mary's Boy.

He was Mary's Son,
And the Son of God was He—
Sent to bring the whole world joy.
There were some who could not hear,
And some were filled with fear—
So they built a Cross
For Mary's Boy.

To His Twelve Disciples
He gave them of His bread.
He gave them to drink of His wine.
*This is my body
And this is my blood,* He said.
*My Cross for you
Will be a sign.*

He went into the garden
And He knelt there to pray.
He said, *Oh, Lord, Thy will be done!*
The soldiers came
And took my Lord away.
They made a Cross
For Mary's Son.

This is my body
And this is my blood!
His body and His blood divine!
He died on the Cross
That my soul should not be lost.

His body and His blood
Redeem mine.

Pastoral

Between the little clouds of heaven
They thought they saw
The Saviour peeping through.
For little tears of heaven
They mistook the gentle dew,
And believed the tiny flowers
That grew upon the plain
To be souvenirs of Jesus,
The Child, come back again.

Little Cats

What happens to little cats?
   Some get drowned in a well,
   Some run over by a car—
   But none goes to hell.

What happens to little cats,
New born, not been here long?
   Some live out their
   Full nine lives—
As mean as they are strong.

Not Else—But

Hip boots
Deep in the blues
(And I never had a hip boot on).
Hair
Blowing back in the wind
(And I never had that much hair).
Diamonds in pawn
(And I never had a diamond
In my natural life).
Me
In the White House
(And ain't never had a black house).
Do, Jesus!
Lord!
Amen!

Tambourines

Tambourines!
Tambourines!
Tambourines
To the glory of God!
Tambourines
To glory!

A gospel shout
And a gospel song:
Life is short
But God is long!

Tambourines!
Tambourines!
Tambourines
To glory!

As Befits a Man

I don't mind dying—
But I'd hate to die all alone!
I want a dozen pretty women
To holler, cry, and moan.

I don't mind dying
But I want my funeral to be fine:
A row of long tall mamas
Fainting, fanning, and crying.

I want a fish-tail hearse
And sixteen fish-tail cars,
A big brass band
And a whole truck load of flowers.

When they let me down,
Down into the clay,
I want the women to holler:
Please don't take him away!
    Ow-ooo-oo-o!
Don't take daddy away!

Maybe

I asked you, baby,
If you understood—
You told me that you didn't,
But you thought you would.

Blue Monday

No use in my going
Downtown to work today,
    It's eight,
    I'm late—
And it's marked down that-a-way.

Saturday and Sunday's
Fun to sport around.
But no use denying—
Monday'll get you down.

That old blue Monday
Will surely get you down.

To Artina

I will take your heart.
I will take your soul out of your body
As though I were God.
I will not be satisfied
With the little words you say to me.
I will not be satisfied
With the touch of your hand
Nor the sweet of your lips alone.
I will take your heart for mine.
I will take your soul.
I will be God when it comes to you.

Uncle Tom

Within—
The beaten pride.
Without—
The grinning face,
The low, obsequious,
Double bow,
The sly and servile grace
Of one the white folks
Long ago
Taught well
To know his
Place.

Abe Lincoln

Well, I know
You had a hard time in your life.
And I know
You knew what hard times meant.
And I guess you understood
That most folks ain't much good,
Also soon as good things come,
They went.
But I think you hoped
Some folks *sometimes* would act
Somewhat according to the fact
That black or white
Ain't just white
Or black.

Imagine

Imagine!
They are afraid of you—
Black dog
That they have kicked
So long.

Imagine!
They are afraid of you—
Monkey
They've laughed at
So long.

Imagine!
They are afraid of you—
Donkey

Driven so long.

Imagine—
Nigger
They are afraid
Of you!

"The Jesus"[1]

Until the crumpets and the christians,
Altars of grass bled paths
From Congo to Cape, shifting sacrificially
Through river beds, shifting
From saberthroat to sand
Voodoo rain drummed juju
Away and spring came,
Came with Galilee
Upon its back to chop
The naked bone of mumbo
Dangling like a dice
Swung from a mirror,
Captain of the stumps of Sir John
Lumped cargoes for Cuba
Among feathered kings rolling
Their skins in flax, moulded
To shaftsteel and psalm.
Through helms of smoke
Balloon dreams of grabber kings
Mooned at groaning girls
Bred on black sheets of seahull.
Was the deacon of pits blessing

---

1. A ship lent to Sir John Hawkins by Queen Elizabeth as support to his business venture in the slave traffic off Cape Verde in the latter half of the sixteenth century.

The mumble of crumbs or
Trying to suck at his knuckles?
In this tambourine of limbs
Where crisscross droves of blackbirds croak
The Jesus weptwashed and slumped
Toward the mines of sugar cane.

Uncollected Poems

1961–1967

If You Would

You could stop the factory whistles blowing,
Stop the mine machines from going,
Stop the atom bombs exploding,
Stop the battleships from loading,
Stop the merchant ships from sailing,
Stop the jail house keys from turning,
Stop the trains from running,
Wheels from rolling where they roll,
   Mouths from eating
   Hearts from beating—
Starve and die to save your soul—
   If you would.
   You could
   If you
   Would.

Encounter

I met You on Your way to death,
Though quite by accident
I chose the path I did,
Not knowing there You went.

When I heard the hooting mob
I started to turn back
But, curious, I stood my ground
Directly in its track
And sickened suddenly
At its sound,
Yet did not
Turn back.

So loud the mob cried,
Yet so weak,
Like a sick and muffled sea.
On Your head You had sharp thorns.
You did not look at me—
But on Your back You carried
My own Misery.

Pair in One

The strangeness
And the stranger
Walk ambiently
Body-rounded:
The life bell
And the death knell
Both at once
Are sounded.

Good Bluffers

Pity all the frightened ones
Who do not *look* afraid—
And so receive no pity from
The ones who make the grade.

Number

When faith in black candles
and in the nothing at all
on clocks runs out
and the time that has gone

and the time to come
is done—
What is the number then
that hasn't yet
been won?
???
??
?

Silent One

This little silent one—
He's all the atoms from the sun
And all the grass blades
From the earth
And all the songs
The heart gives birth
To when the throat
Stops singing—
He's my son—
This little
Silent
One.

doorknobs

The simple silly terror
of a doorknob on a door
that turns to let in life
on two feet standing,
walking, talking,
wearing dress or trousers,
maybe drunk or maybe sober,

maybe smiling, laughing, happy,
maybe tangled in the terror
of a yesterday past grandpa
when the door from out there opened
into here where I, antenna,
recipient of your coming,
received the talking image
of the simple silly terror
of a door that opens
at the turning of a knob
to let in life
walking, talking, standing
wearing dress or trousers,
drunk or maybe sober,
smiling, laughing, happy,
or tangled in the terror
of a yesterday past grandpa
not of our own doing.

We, Too

Oh, Congo brother
With your tribal marks,
We, too, emerge
From ageless darks.
We, too, emit
A frightening cry
From body scarred,
Soul that won't die.
We encarnadine the sky.
We, who have no
Tribal marks to bear,
Bear in our souls
The great welts there

That years have cut
Through skin and lashed
Through bone
In silent cry,
In unheard moan—
We, too,
Congo brother,
Rise with you.

For Russell and Rowena Jelliffe

And so the seed
Becomes a flower
And in its hour
Reproduces dreams
And flowers.

And so the root
Becomes a trunk
And then a tree
And seeds of trees
And springtime sap
And summer shade
And autumn leaves
And shape of poems
And dreams—
And more than tree.

And so it is
With those who make
Of life a flower,
A tree, a dream
Reproducing (on into
Its own and mine

And your infinity)
Its beauty and its life
In you and me.

And so it was
And is with you:
The seed, the flower,
The root, the tree,
The dream, the you.

This poem I make

(From poems you made)

For you.

Dream of Freedom

There is a dream in the land
With its back against the wall.
By muddled names and strange
Sometimes the dream is called.

There are those who claim
This dream for theirs alone—
A sin for which we know
They must atone.

Unless shared in common
Like sunlight and like air,
The dream will die for lack
Of substance anywhere.

The dream knows no frontier or tongue,
The dream no class or race.

The dream cannot be kept secure
In any one locked place.

This dream today embattled,
With its back against the wall—
To save the dream for one
It must be saved for ALL—
Our dream of freedom!

Small Memory

I have this
Strange small memory
Of death
And seven trees
And winds that have
No ecstasies
To search
And find
And search
And find
The search
That is
Not mine.

Drums

I dream of the drums
And remember
Nights without stars in Africa.

Remember, remember, remember!

I dream of the drums
And remember

Slave ships, billowing sails,
The Western Ocean,
And the landing at Jamestown.

Remember, remember, remember!

I dream of drums
And recall, like a picture,
Congo Square in New Orleans—
Sunday—the slaves' one day of "freedom"—
The juba-dance in Congo Square.

I dream of the drums
And hear again
Jelly Roll's piano,
Buddy Bolden's trumpet,
Kid Ory's trombone,
St. Cyr's banjo,
They join the drums . . .
And I remember.

Jazz!

I dream of the drums
And remember.

Africa!
The ships!
New shore
And drums!

Remember!
I remember!
Remember!

Chicago

It is not Lake Michigan's lapping waves,
Dun-colored without glow,
Nor the scorching summers and freezing winters
Where the lake winds blow,
Nor the elevated trains that coil,
Nor the uncoiled lines of cars
That stretch to the very prairie's edge
When "time to quit" drops go-home bars,
It's not the stockyards' hearty stench
Delicate on the breeze,
Nor the gamblers' dice
Nor the sinners' vice
Nor the righteous on their knees,
And it's not the Civic Opera
Nor the Wrigley Building's light
Nor Marshall Field's
Or the Merchandise Mart
Or the bars that blaze at night,
And it's not the memory of Al Capone
Or Sandburg or McCormick
Or Harriet Monroe
Or Mrs. Potter Palmer.
Armour, Swift,
Insul or DuSable—Negro—
Or any names we know—
But it's *all* the names
In the phone book,
Their relatives and friends
And Pa's and Ma's and Grandpa's
Back generations to other nations
That sent the names
With un-anglo spellings.
The faces with un-anglo shapes,

The skins not always white
And the tongues not always English
And the polyglot hands
And the polyglot ways
To make headline nights and headline days
That flash beyond the Wrigley light
And forge of Chicago a sun not a moon—
But a *sun* that blazes and turns and glows
And lightens and brightens
All orbits beyond its looped center
And lake bordered edge
And prairie backdrop
And motorized cop
And multi-ranged sky
And the image of God
   Chicago!
That's found in its eye:

Old Age

Having known robins on the window sill
And loves over which to grieve,
What can you dream of now
In which you still believe?

Having known snow in winter
And the burst of blooms in spring,
What can you seek now
To make your heart still sing?

If there should be nothing new,
Might not the self-same wonders do?
And if there should be nothing old,
Might not new wonders still unfold?

Should nothing new or old appeal,
Still friends will ask,
"How do you feel?"

To You

To sit and dream, to sit and read,
To sit and learn about the world
Outside our world of here and now—
    our problem world—
To dream of vast horizons of the soul
Through dreams made whole,
Unfettered free—help me!
All you who are dreamers, too,
Help me make our world anew.
I reach out my hands to you.

Not What Was

By then the poetry is written
and the wild rose of the world
blooms to last so short a time
before its petals fall.
The air is music
and its melody a spiral
until it widens
beyond the tip of time
and so is lost
to poetry and the rose—
belongs instead to vastness beyond form,
to universe that nothing can contain,
to unexplored space
which sends no answers back

to fill the vase unfilled
or spread in lines
upon another page—
that anyhow was never written
because the thought could not escape
the place in which it bloomed
before the rose had gone.

Christmas Eve: Nearing Midnight in New York

The Christmas trees are almost all sold
And the ones that are left go cheap.
The children almost all over town
Have almost gone to sleep.

The skyscraper lights on Christmas Eve
Have almost all gone out.
There's very little traffic,
Almost no one about.

Our town's almost as quiet
As Bethlehem must have been
Before a sudden angel chorus
Sang PEACE ON EARTH!
GOOD WILL TO MEN!

Our old Statue of Liberty
Looks down almost with a smile
As the Island of Manhattan
Awaits the morning of the Child.

Metropolitan Museum

I came in from the roar
Of city streets
To look upon a Grecian urn.

I thought of Keats—
To mind came verses
Filled with lovers' sweets.

Out of ages past there fell
Into my hands the petals
Of an asphodel.

Emperor Haile Selassie
On Liberation Day, May 5, 1966

That he is human . . . and living . . .
And of our time . . .
Makes it seem a miracle
All the more sublime
That he becomes a symbol
Of our Negritude,
Our dignity . . . and food
On which men who are neither
Kings of Kings nor Lions of Judah
Yet may feed their pride . . .
And live to hope for that great day
When all mankind is one
And each is king in common
Of all his eyes survey.
And each man shares
The strength derived from head held high . . .
And holds his head, King of Kings . . .

Our symbol of a dream
That will not die.

Suburban Evening

A dog howled.
Weird became the night.
No good reason
For my fright—
But reason often
May play host
To quiet
Unreasonable
Ghosts.

Demonstration

Did you ever walk into a firehose
With the water turned up full blast?
Did you ever walk toward police guns
When each step might be your last?
Did you ever stand up in the face of snarling dogs
And not move as the dogs came?
Did you ever feel the tear gas burn
Your day, your night, your dawn?
   Your dawn
When the water's a rainbow hue,
   Your dawn
When the guns are no longer aimed at you,
   Your dawn
When the cops forget their jails,
   Your dawn
When the police dogs wag their tails,

Your dawn
When the tear-gas canisters are dry,
   Your dawn
When you own the star in the sky,
   Your dawn
When the atom bomb is yours—
   Your dawn
When you have the keys to all doors—
   Your dawn
Will you ever forget *your dawn?*

Bitter Brew

Whittle me down
To a strong thin reed
With a piercing tip
To match my need.

Spin me out
To a tensile wire
To derrick the stones
Of my problems higher.

Then simmer me slow
In the freedom cup
Till only an essence
Is left to sup.

May that essence be
The black poison of me
To give the white bellies
The third degree:

Concocted by history
Brewed by fate—

A bitter concentrate
   Of hate.

Freedom

Some folks think
By burning churches
They burn
Freedom.
Some folks think
By imprisoning me
They imprison
Freedom.
Some folks think
By killing a man
They kill
Freedom.
But Freedom
Stands up and laughs
In their faces
And says,
No—
Not so!
No!

Flotsam

On the shoals of Nowhere,
Cast up—my boat,
Bow all broken,
No longer afloat.

On the shoals of Nowhere,
Wasted—my song—
Yet taken by the sea wind
And blown along.

Appendix

Poems Circulated by the
Associated Negro Press

Song of the Refugee Road

Refugee road, refugee road
Where do I go from here?
Weary my feet! Heavy the road!
My heart is filled with fear.
The ones I left far behind—
    Home nowhere!
Dark winds of trouble moan through my mind.
    None to care!
Bitter my past! Tomorrow—What's there?
Refugee road! Refugee road!
Where do I go from here?
Walking down the refugee road.
Must I beg? Must I steal?
Must I lie? Must I kneel?
Or driven like dumb war-weary sheep,
Must we wander the high road and weep?
Or will the world listen to my appeal?
From China where the war gods thunder and roar.
From all the dark lands where freedom is no more.
Vienna, city of light and gladness,
Once gay with waltzes, now bowed in sadness.
Dark Ethiopia, stripped of her mirth.
Spain, where the shells plant steel seeds in the earth.
Oh, Statue of Liberty, lighting tomorrow,
Look! And have pity on my sorrow:
    Home nowhere! None to care!
    Bitter my past! Tomorrow—what's there?
    Refugee road! Refugee road!
    Where do I go from here?
    Walking down the refugee road.

America's Young Black Joe!

One tenth of the population
Of this mighty nation
Was sun-tanned by nature long ago,
But we're Americans by birth and training
So our country will be gaining
When every citizen learns to know
That I'm America's Young Black Joe!

Manly, good natured, smiling and gay,
My sky is sometimes cloudy
But it won't stay that way.
I'm comin', I'm comin'—
But my head AIN'T bending, low!
I'm walking proud! I'm speaking out loud!
I'm America's Young Black Joe!

This is my own my native land,
And I'm mighty glad that's true.
Land where my fathers worked
The same as yours worked, too.
So from every mountain side
Let freedom's bright torch glow—
Standing hand in hand with democracy,
I'm America's Young Black Joe!

Besides Joe Louis there's Henry Armstrong,
Three titles to his name,
Beat everybody that was his size
In the fighting game.
Then there was Kenny Washington
In a football suit,
Run, pass, kick, tackle, and block to boot.

And don't forget track men like Ellerbe
Who piles up points for Tuskegee,
Or Jessie Owens with his laurel wreath
That made old Hitler grit his teeth.
Look at those dark boys streaking by,
Feet just flying and head held high.
Looky yonder at Metcalf, Johnson,
Tolan! Down the field they go,
Swift and proud before the crowd—
They're America's Young Black Joe!

This is our own, our native land,
And I'm mighty glad that's true.
Land where my fathers worked
The same as yours worked, too.
So from every mountain side
Let freedom's bright torch glow—
Standing hand in hand with democracy
I'm America's Young Black Joe!

Ballad of the Fool

Poor, poor fool!
No sense at all.
Best he can do's
Walk around and not fall.

He don't have no place except
Up and down the block
In what's happening to the world
He takes no stock.

He just sits and grins
And laughs in the sun

And looks like
He's having fun.

He don't know there is a war.
He ain't on WPA.
Gee! Sometimes I wish I
Was a fool that way.

Ballad of Walter White

Now Walter White
Is mighty light.
Being a colored man
Who looks like white,
He can go down South
Where a lynching takes place
And the white folks never
Guess his race—
So he investigates
To his heart's desire
Whereas if he was brownskin
They'd set him on fire!
By being himself
Walter finds out
What them lynchers
Was all about.
But back to New York
Before going to press—
Cause if the crackers ever got him
There'd be one Negro less!
Yes, it's our good fortune
He was born so light
Cause it's swell to have a leader
That can pass for white.

The Mitchell Case

I see by the papers
Where Mitchell's won his case.
Down South the railroads now
Must give us equal space.
Even if we're rich enough
   To want a Pullman car,
The Supreme Court says we get it—
And a diner and a bar!
Now since the Court in Washington
Can make a rule like that,
If we went to court enough we might
Get Jim Crow on the mat
And pin his shoulders to the ground
And drive him from the land—
Since the Constitution ain't enough—
To protect a colored man—
And we have to go to court to make
The crackers understand.
But for poor people
It's kinder hard to sue.
Mr. Mitchell, you did right well—
But the rest of us ain't you.
Seems to me it would be simpler
If the Government would declare
They're tired of all this Jim Crow stuff
And just give it the air.
Seems to me it's time to realize
That in the U.S.A.
To have Jim Crow's too Hitler-like
In this modern age and day—
Cause fine speeches sure sound hollow
About Democracy
When all over America,

They still Jim Crowing me.
To earn a dollar sometimes
Is hard enough to do—
Let alone having to take that dollar
To go and sue!

Explain It, Please

I see by the papers
What seems mighty funny to me.
The British are fighting for freedom
But India ain't free.
The colored weeklies tell me
In the British colonies
The white man stands on his two feet
But the black man's on his knees.
And they tell me that in Africa
The color line's drawn tight,
So when the English holler freedom
Can it be that they are right?
Course there's a mighty lot of fog and smoke,
But I'm trying hard to see
How folks can have a mouth full of freedom—
And a handful of dung for me.

Ballad of the Black Sheep

My brother,
He never left the old fireside.
I was the one
Who liked to ride.

I always felt I
Had to wander and roam.
Never met nobody's got
What it takes to keep me home.

Every job I have
I throw away my pay
And raise sand each and
Every day.

My brother gathers
What the folks call
Moss.
But me—
I am a
Total loss.

Help me, Jesus!

Epitaph

Uncle Tom,
When he was alive,
Filled the white folks
Full of jive.
But the trouble was
His jive was bad.
Now, thank God,
Uncle Tom
Is dead.

So Tired Blues

I'm gonna wake up some mornin'
With the sun in my hand.
Gonna throw the sun
Way across the land—
 Cause I'm tired,
 Tired as I can be.

Gonna throw the sun
In somebody's face
 Recreate
 The human race—
  Cause I'm tired,
  Tired as I can be.

When the sunstroke strikes,
Gonna rise and shine,
Take this world and
Make it mine—
 Cause I'm tired,
 Tired as I can be.

Don't try to figger
Out these words I sing.
They'll keep you figgerin'
To way next spring—
 Cause I'm tired,
 Tired as I can be.

Return to Sea

Today I go back to the sea
And the wind-beaten rise of the foam.
Today I go back to the sea
And it's just as though I was home.

It's just as though I was home again
On this ship of iron and steam.
It's just as though I'd found again
The broken edge of a dream.

Jazz Girl

Jazz?
Remember that song
About the wind in the trees
Singing me pretty melodies?
Was nice, wasn't it?
Hear that violin?
Say, Buddy, you know
It's spring in the country
Where flowers grow.
Play, jazz band! Play!
I'm tired! Oh, gee!
Sure, go ahead,
Buy a drink for me.

Pathological Puzzle

There are so many diseases
From rabies to the wheezes
That people can contract
Till it's hard to understand
   How any man
   remains intact.

Dixie Man to Uncle Sam

How can you
Shake a fist at tyranny
Everywhere else
But here?

Do you not see?
I, too, in Dixie
Stand in need
Of being free:

Jim Crow's
Too Hitler-like
For you—
Or me.

Governor Fires Dean

I see by the papers
Where Governor Talmadge get real mad
Cause one of Georgia's teachers
Thinks Democracy ain't bad.
The Governor has done had him

Kicked plumb out of school
Just because that teacher
Believes the Golden Rule.
Governor Talmadge says that white folks
And black folks cannot mix
Unless they want to put
The sovereign State of Georgia
In an awful kind of fix.
The Governor says equality
(Even just in education)
Is likely to lead us all
Right straight to ruination—
So I reckon Governor Talmadge
Must be a Hitler man
Cause that's just what Hitler'd say
If he ruled the land.
Ain't it funny how some white folks
Have the strangest way
Of acting just like Hitler
In the U.S.A.?

Get Up Off That Old Jive

White folks,
You better get some new jive.
That old jive is wearing thin.
I been listening to that old jive
Since I don't know when.

Fact of the matter,
To tell you the truth
Instead of just words
I want action to boot.

You been making fine speeches
For a long long while
Now give some democracy
To each brown-skin child.

A war's taking place.
We ain't fighting for fun.
We're fighting to win—
This fight's got to be won.

We want just what
The president said:
    Freedom from fear,
    And from want—
    To be men,
    And have bread.

So get up off that old jive.
Let's start clearing the way:
Put an end to Jim Crow
Right now, today.

A man can fight
Better that way.

Fourth of July Thought

Remember on our far-flung fronts
This Fourth of July,
Soldiers of Democracy
Guard our earth and sky.

Those of us who stay at home
Have grave duties, too:
    The WAR FRONT

Depends on
THE HOME FRONT—
The HOME FRONT is YOU!

Battle Ground

The soldier said to the general,
General, what shall I shoot?
The general said, Man, shoot your gun—
And you better shoot straight to boot.
The soldier said to the general,
What shall my target be?
The general said, Man, I don't care,
Just so your target ain't me!
The soldier said to the general,
I can't see nothing but space,
Yet every time I lift my head
The bullets pass my face.
The general said to the soldier,
You do not need to see
Who you're fighting nor what for.
Just take your orders from me.
The soldier said to the general,
They shootin' in front and behind.
The general said to the soldier,
Don't pay them bullets no mind.
The soldier said, Then, general,
Why don't YOU come out here with me?
The general said, That isn't right
Cause I'm the general! See?

Joe Louis

Joe Louis is a man
For men to imitate—
When this country needed him,
He did not stall or fail.

Joe took up the challenge
And joined up for war.
Nobody had to ask him,
"What are you waiting for?"

As a private in the army
Of his talents he gave free
Two mighty boxing matches
To raise funds for liberty.

That's more than lots of others
Who still try to jim-crow Joe
Have either heart or mind to do—
So this is to let them know

That Joe Louis is a man for any
    man to imitate.
If everybody was like Joe Louis
    there'd be no
"Too little" or "too late."

Crow Goes, Too

Uncle Sam—
And old Jim Crow—
Right along with you
Wherever you go.

Done gone to England
Took Jim Crow there—
But England don't like
The feathers you wear.

Driberg in Commons
The other day
Said, kindly take that
Bird away.

Uncle Sam,
Why don't you get hep?
Stop marching with
A Jim Crow step.

This is a war
To free all men.
Throw Jim Crow out—
And let decency in.
That's the way
To win!

Lonely Nocturne

When dawn lights the sky
And day and night meet,
I climb my stairs high
Above the grey street.
I lift my window
To look at the sky
Where moon kisses star
Goodbye.

When dawn lights the sky
I seek my lonely room.

The halls as I go by
Echo like a tomb.
And I wonder why
As I take out my key,
There is nobody there
But me—
When dawn lights the sky.

Troubled Water

Between us, always, loved one,
There lies this troubled water.
You are my sky, my shining sun
Over troubled water.

I journey far to touch your hand.
The trip is troubled water.
We see yet cannot understand
This fateful troubled water.

Deep hearts, dear, dream of happiness
Balked by troubled water.
Between us always—love, and this—
This sea of troubled water.

Total War

The reason Dixie
Is so mean today
Is because it wasn't licked
In the proper way.
And I reckon old Hitler
A cracker must be—

Because he, too,
Wants to Jim Crow me.

So I'm in favor of beating
Hitler to his knees—
Then beating him some more
Until he hollers, Please!

Cause if we let our enemies
Breathe again—
They're liable to live
To be another pain.

Gandhi Is Fasting

Mighty Britain, tremble!
Let your empire's standard sway
Lest it break entirely—
Mr. Gandhi fasts today.

You may think it foolish—
That there's no truth in what I say—
That all of Asia's watching
As Gandhi fasts today.

All of Asia's watching,
And I am watching, too,
For I am also jim crowed—
As India is jim crowed by you.

You know quite well, Great Britain,
That it is not right
To starve and beat and oppress
Those who are not white.

Of course, we do it too,
Here in the U.S.A.
May Gandhi's prayers help us, as well,
As he fasts today.

Judge William Hastie

Now you take
This Bill Hastie guy—
He resigned
And told the world why;
He can't see why
Colored boys can't fly!
And neither do I.

What I Think

The guys who own
The biggest guns
Are the lucky ones
These days.
Being hip
To your marksmanship
Is what pays.
On the other hand
There's some demand
For a world plan.
Some folks wish
The human race might
Try to do right—
Instead of just fight.
But others still feel
That any old heel

Has a right
To laissez faire
Anywhere,
And that Empire's right.
As for me,
I can't agree,
To my nose colonies stink.
People ought to be FREE
And have liberty—
That's what I think.

Just an Ordinary Guy

He's just an ordinary guy.
He doesn't occupy
A seat of government
Or anything like that.

He works hard every day,
Saturday brings home his pay—
He may take a glass of beer
Sometimes at that.

He never had his name in lights,
He's never front page news.
He stands up for his rights,
Yet doesn't beef or sing the blues.

But when his country gets in trouble
And it's time to fight and die,
He doesn't ask for a deferment—
He's just an ordinary guy.

Listen, Hitler!
About this ordinary guy,

You may wonder why
He's taken such an awful
Hate to you.

But you'll never understand
His kind of man.
You won't need to—
You'll be dead when he gets through.

He doesn't bully or act rough.
You never hear him bluff.
But there's one thing certain, Nazi,
He won't stand for your type of stuff.

He just doesn't like the idea
Of men being in a cage,
And the way you try to boss folks
Puts him in a rage.

You've got the whole round world in trouble
With your boastings and your lies.
But you'll never beat us, Hitler—
Not us ordinary guys!

Speaking of Food

I hear folks talking
About coffee's hard to get,
And they don't know how
They're going to live without it.

I hear some others saying
They can't buy no meat to fry,
And the way they say it
You'd think they're gonna die.

If I was to sit down
And write to Uncle Sam,
I'll tell him that I reckon
I can make it without ham.

I'd say, "Feed those fighting forces
For they're the ones today
That need to have their victuals
To wipe our foes away!"

Looks to me
That's what we ought to say.

Puzzlement

I don't know why
They're so hard on me and you?
We don't do nothing in the jook joints
Rich folks don't do.

But the rich folks have clubs
And licenses and such,
Only trouble is, we
Can't afford that much.

The Bells Toll Kindly

Many clocks in many towers
Have struck for me delightful hours.
Many cities, many towns
Have gathered laughter,
Scattered frowns.
Many clocks in many towers
Have laughed their hours.

Some day in some higher tower
A clock will strike its final hour.
When it tolls I shall go
Not wishing that the hour be slow.

I shall then remember still
How it struck one gay December
Near the Kremlin white with snow
And the midnight a warm ember
Of love's glow.

I shall then still sweet recall
How one evening in Les Halles
We walked together arm in arm
Hearing Notre Dame's grave charm.

Then I shall still realize
How, round the world, the bells are wise,
So when I hear that last bell toll,
Willingly, I'll bare my soul.

For many clocks in many towers,
Have struck for me delightful hours,
So there shall be no need to fear
The final hour drawing near.

Madam and the Crime Wave

I said, I believe
This world's gone mad,
Never heard of folks
Acting so bad.

Last night a man
Knocked a woman down,

Robbed her and raped her
On the ground.

Such a fate, folks say,
Is worse than death!
When I read it
I held my breath.

With your money gone
Where is death's sting?
(Course you always got
That other thing.)

Madam's Christmas (or Merry Christmas Everybody)

I forgot
to send a card to Jennie
But the truth about cousins is
There's too many.

I also forgot
A card for Joe
But I believe I'll let
The old rascal go.

I disremembered
My old friend Jack
But he's been evil
Long as he's been black.

I done bought
Four boxes now,
And I can't afford
No more nohow.

So MERRY CHRISTMAS
Everybody!
Cards or no cards
Here's HOWDY!

Song after Lynching

I guess DEMOCRACY'S meant to be
Just a high-flown sound
Flying around . . .
Cause the crackers get mad
If I try to pin it down.

I guess LIBERTY'S supposed
To be just a hope.
When Negroes try to make it real
They look for a rope.

White folks oughtn't to use
Those fine words that way
When they don't mean a thing
Those words say . . .

Getting on the radio
About DEMOCRACY'S star . . .
And herded up
In a Jim Crow car!

Speeches like theirs
Puzzle me.
JUSTICE don't jibe
With a lynching tree.

Bonds for All

Buy a Bond for Grandma—
Grandma's growing old.
Buy a Bond for Baby—
Bless his little soul.

Buy a Bond for Papa,
Though it's Father's Day.
Buy a Bond for Mama
To salt away.

Buy a Bond for Uncle.
Get one for Auntie, too.
Then buy one for your Buddy
Who's fighting for you.

BACK THE ATTACK
Is the slogan this fall.
Back it, Mr. Citizen,
With War Bonds for all.

Poor Girl's Ruination

I went to Chicago
At the age of three.
Chicago nearly
Ruined me.

I went to Detroit
At twenty-one.
What Chicago started
Detroit's done.

If I'd a-growed up
With a little money
I might not a-been
Ruined, honey.

Before you give
A girl damnation,
Take what is in
Consideration.

Poem to Uncle Sam

Uncle Sam
With old Jim Crow—
Like a shadow
Right behind you—
Everywhere
You go.

Uncle Sam,
Why don't you
Turn around,
And before you
Tackle Hitler—
Shoot Jim down?

Song of Adoration

I would like to be a white man, wouldn't you?
There's so many lovely things that I could do.
   I could lynch a Negro—
   And never go to jail, you know,
I would love to be a white man, wouldn't you?

I would love to be a white man, wouldn't you?
So many tasty things that I could do.
　　I could tell the starving Indian nation
　　To go straight to damnation,
Oh, I would love to be a white man, wouldn't you?

I would love to be a white man, wouldn't you?
There's such intriguing things that one could do.
　　I could say to Stalin, listen kid,
　　You're just an Asiatic mongrel Red.
Ah, I would love to be a white man, wouldn't you?

I would love to be a white woman also, too.
There's so many cultural things that I could do.
　　I could belong to the D.A.R.
　　Tell Marian Anderson, stay . . . out the D.A.R.!
I could ADORE being a white woman, wouldn't you?

I'd love to be a white congressman, too.
There's so many helpful things I could do.
　　Just to get the Negro's goat
　　I wouldn't let NO soldiers vote.
I would love to be a white congressman, wouldn't you?

Oh, I'd love to be a white Christian, ain't it true.
I'd act just like my fellow Christians do.
　　For Jesus I would search
　　With no black folks in my church.
Amen, I'd love to be a white man, wouldn't you?
　　Halleloo! . . . O Halleloo . . .
　　Hallelloo-o-o

Bonds: In Memoriam

Written Especially for the Writers' War Board, War Loan Drive, by
Langston Hughes (For ANP)

Eddie and Charlie and Jack and Ted
And Harry and Arthur and Ken
   Have all gone down
   Where heroes are found
In the land of the lost fighting men.

Eddie and Charlie and Ted and Ken
And Harry and Arthur and Jack
   All fought well
   Through a living hell
To a land where there's no coming back.

But Eddie and Charlie and Ted and Ken
And all the men who are gone
   Still look to you
   To see it through—
The least you can do is buy a Bond.

The least you can do is do your job well—
They fought that your future'd be sunny.
   These men who gave all
   That our cause might not fall
Only ask that you lend your money.

Worriation

There's something disturbing
To a cat, no doubt,
Seeing birds with wings
Flying about.

Is there something disturbing
To Aryans in the way
That Negroes, being black,
Keep looking that way?

Ballad of Harry Moore

(Killed at Mims, Florida, on Christmas night, 1951)

Florida means land of flowers.
It was on Christmas night
In the state named for the flowers
Men came bearing dynamite.

Men came stealing through the orange groves
Bearing hate instead of love,
While the Star of Bethlehem
Was in the sky above.

Oh, memories of a Christmas evening
When Wise Men travelled from afar
Seeking out a lowly manger
Guided by a Holy Star!

Oh, memories of a Christmas evening
When to Bethlehem there came
"Peace on earth, good will to men"—
Jesus was His name.

But they must've forgotten Jesus
Down in Florida that night
Stealing through the orange groves
Bearing hate and dynamite.

It was a little cottage,
A family, name of Moore.

In the windows wreaths of holly,
And a pine wreath on the door.

Christmas, 1951,
The family prayers were said
When father, mother, daughter,
And grandmother went to bed.

The father's name was Harry Moore.
The N.A.A.C.P.
Told him to carry out its work
That Negroes might be free.

So it was that Harry Moore
(So deeply did he care)
Sought the right for men to live
With their heads up everywhere.

Because of that, white killers,
Who like Negroes "in their place,"
Came stealing through the orange groves
On that night of dark disgrace.

It could not be in Jesus' name,
Beneath the bedroom floor,
On Christmas night the killers
Hid the bomb for Harry Moore.

It could not be in Jesus' name
The killers took his life,
Blew his home to pieces
And killed his faithful wife.

It could not be for the sake of love
They did this awful thing—
For when the bomb exploded
No hearts were heard to sing.

And certainly no angels cried,
"Peace on earth, good will to men"—
But around the world an echo hurled
A question: When? . . . When? . . . When?

When will men for sake of peace
And for democracy
Learn no bombs a man can make
Keep men from being free?

It seems that I hear Harry Moore.
From the earth his voice cries,
No bomb can kill the dreams I hold—
For freedom never dies!

I will not stop! I will not stop—
For freedom never dies!
I will not stop! I will not stop!
Freedom never dies!

So should you see our Harry Moore
Walking on a Christmas night,
Don't run and hide, you killers,
He has no dynamite.

In his heart is only love
For all the human race,
And all he wants is for every man
To have his rightful place.

And this he says, our Harry Moore,
As from the grave he cries:
No bomb can kill the dreams I hold
For freedom never dies!

Freedom never dies, I say!
Freedom never dies!

Message to the President

Mr. President, kindly please,
May I have a word with you?
There's one thing for a long time,
I've been wishing you would do.
In your fireside chats on the radio
I hear you telling the world
What you want them to know,
And your speeches in general
Sound mighty fine,
But there's one thing, Mr. President,
That worries my mind.
I hear you talking about freedom
  For the Finn,
  The Jew,
  And the Czechoslovak—
But you never seem to mention
Us folks who're black!
We're all Americans, Mr. President,
And I've had enough
Of putting up with this
Jim Crow stuff.
I want the self-same rights
Other Americans have today.
I want to fly a plane
Like any other man may.
I don't like this Jim Crow army
Or this Jim Crow navy,
Or the lily-white marines
Licking up the gravy.
We're one-tenth of the nation,
Mr. President, fourteen million strong.
If you help to keep us down,

You're wrong.
We work and pay our taxes.
Our patriotism's good.
We try to live like
Decent Americans should.
That's why as citizens, Mr. President,
We have the right to demand
The next time you make a speech,
Take an all-out stand
And make your meaning
Just as clear to me
As you do when talking to
Those Englishmen across the sea.
Since, for our land's defense
If we have to fight—
We ought to be together,
Black and white.
So what I'm asking, Mr. President,
Is to hear you say
No more segregation in the U.S.A.
And when you mention the Finns,
    And the Jew,
    And the Czechoslovak,
Don't forget the fourteen million
Here who're black.
Such a speech, Mr. President, for me
Would put a whole lot more meaning
In Democracy.
So next time you sit down
To that radio,
Just like you lambast Hitler,
Give Jim Crow a blow—
For all I'm asking, Mr. President,
Is to hear you say,

No more segregation in the U.S.A.
My friends, NO more
Segregation in the U.S.A.

Promised Land

The Promised Land
Is always just ahead.
You will not reach it
Ere you're dead.

But your children's children
By their children will be led
To a spot from which the Land—
Still lies ahead.

Chicago Blues

(moral: go slow)

Chicago is a town
That sure do run on wheels.
Runs so fast you don't know
How good the ground feels.

I got in town on Monday
Tuesday rolling drunk
Wednesday morning
I pawned my trunk.

Thursday morning
Cutting aces high
My stock went up
Head in the sky.

Friday riding
In a Cadillac,
She said, Daddy, you can ride
Long as you stay black.

Saturday I said, Baby,
You been good to me—
But I'm no one-woman man,
I need two or three.

Sunday I was living
In a ten room flat
Monday I was back
Where I started at.

Chicago is a town
That sure do run on wheels
Runs so fast you don't know
How good the ground feels.

Index of First Lines

Index of Titles

Cumulative Index of First Lines

A dog howled., **3**:258
A girl with all that raising, **2**:58
A little Southern colored child, **2**:146
A man knocked three times., **2**:170
A nigger comes home from work:, **2**:198
A slash of the wrist, **1**:166
A wild poppy-flower, **2**:118
A woman standing in the doorway, **3**:69
A wonderful time—the War:, **3**:42
Ah, **1**:44
Albert!, **1**:98
All day in the sun, **1**:120
All day subdued, polite, **2**:192
All day Sunday didn't even dress up., **2**:26
All life is but the climbing of a hill, **1**:251
All over the world, **2**:242
All the craziness, **3**:228
All the tom-toms of the jungles beat in my
    blood, **1**:57
An old Negro minister concludes his
    sermon in his loudest voice, **2**:177
. . . and here is, **3**:167
And so, **3**:174
And so the seed, **3**:249
Anybody, **2**:119
Arabella Johnson and the Texas Kid, **2**:43
As if it were some noble thing, **3**:164
As though her lips, **2**:267
At de feet o' Jesus, **1**:93
At the back fence calling, **2**:262
Aunt Sue has a head full of stories., **1**:40
Awake all night with loving, **2**:66

Baby, how come you can't see me, **3**:33
Baby, if you love me, **2**:62
Bear in mind, **1**:120
Beat the drums of tragedy for me., **1**:34
Because my mouth, **1**:171
Because you are to me a song, **1**:184
Been workin' on de levee, **2**:39
Beige sailors with large noses, **2**:182

Being walkers with the dawn and morning,
    1:162
Bernice said she wanted, **2**:56
Better in the quiet night, **1**:169
Between the little clouds of heaven, **3**:234
Between two rivers, **3**:77
Between us, always, loved one, **3**:280
Big Ben, I'm gonna bust you bang up side
    the wall!, **2**:25
Big Boy came, **2**:281
Big Buddy, Big Buddy, **2**:91
Black, **2**:95
Black smoke of sound, **1**:261
Blood, **3**:201
Booker T., **3**:212
Bring me all of your dreams, **1**:55
Buy a Bond for Grandma—, **3**:289
By then the poetry is written, **3**:255
By what sends, **3**:162

Cabaret, cabaret!, **1**:100
Carried lonely up the aisle, **2**:211
Carried me to de court, **1**:86
Cause you don't love me, **1**:98
Cheap little rhymes, **3**:72
Chicago is a town, **3**:298
Children, I come back today, **1**:220
Chile, these steps is hard to climb.,
    3:67
Christ is a nigger, **3**:155
Cinnamon and rayon, **2**:214
Clean the spittoons, boy., **1**:82
Clutching at trees and clawing rocks, **1**:183
Colored child, **3**:183
Columbia, **1**:230
Come, **1**:42
Come now, all you who are singers, **1**:141
Comrade Lenin of Russia, **1**:140
Consider me, **3**:198
Corners, **2**:216
Could be Hastings Street, **2**:205

Cumulative Index of Titles

"Riley